Tampa's STORY

Tampa's STORY

*How I was lucky enough to be adopted by
The World's Most Perfect Dog*

CHRISTIE FLETCHER

MCP BOOKS

MCP Books
2301 Lucien Way #415
Maitland, FL 32751
407·339·4217
www.MCPBooks.com

© 2018 by Christie Fletcher

Printed in the United States of America
Edited by Mill City Press.

ISBN-13: 9781545634226

TABLE OF CONTENTS

To Tampa,

This is for you. My best friend.

From the time you were just a puppy, you were dedicated to spending your life giving to everyone you met. There was never a fearful, mean, or selfish bone in your body.

Your journey began with me, and I thank God every day that you landed on my back porch that warm summer morning.

I learned courage, compassion, and forgiveness from you that I never even realized existed. You filled my heart with joy and hope, and then led me on a beautiful path to share that spirit that shined inside you.

Thank you for your smile, your soft ears, your loving doggie kisses, and the strength you gave me to keep pressing on when times seemed very dark.

You were the bright, warm light of my life.

Now it is my turn to keep that glorious light shining by telling your story.

Spread your wings, my beautiful angel. I know you are watching over all of us.

And when my journey here is finished, I look forward to seeing you again.

Because Tampa was all about spreading love around, a portion of the proceeds from his book will be going to animal shelters and rescues in need of help.

INTRODUCTION

"Where in the world did you find him?"

The vet tech sitting behind the counter hopped up out of her chair and peeked over to get a closer look. Her face lit up with a glowing smile.

Tampa's oversized tan puppy paws were all aligned in a perfect sit position. His ears were forward, and his soft brown eyes were sparkling as he smiled back at her. It was his first puppy checkup.

"I didn't find him. He found me."

He had been in my life for only a month or so, and I already knew what a lucky girl I was. It's that wonderful thing called grace. I was blessed with something very special that only happens once in a lifetime. He was here to make a difference.

I hope, as you are reading this, that you are one of the fortunate ones who met him. You will know exactly what I am talking about. You would have seen how he shined! And you would have felt his warmth and love as you looked into his eyes and felt his soft coat, embracing everything he had to give. He touched people's lives, making memories everywhere he went. He saved dogs' lives. And he certainly changed mine by opening wonderful new doors that I would never have ventured through without him.

If you never met him, then say hello now. Say hello to Tampa—The World's Most Perfect Dog. A good friend of mine gave him that title one day as we were spending time with all of our dogs together, and it just stuck. The more people he met, the more he continued to prove that is just what he was.

He wore the name well as we learned the fascinating world of search and rescue, as we reached people through pet therapy, and as we worked as partners to help troubled shelter dogs in desperate need of a new life.

The beauty of his life is that Tampa did not care about perfection. He just cared. We could all learn from that. It isn't that he never did anything wrong. There is no such being. It's just that he found the most important times in life to do everything right. And that is what the real journey is all about.

Here is his story.

CHAPTER 1

THE MOMENT WE MET

My very first memory is of two Dumbo-sized ears and a fluffy black-and-tan tail sticking up, gently wagging. He was trying to stretch his wet nose up high enough to see over the covered part of the screen door in the back of our house. I giggled a little at the sight of a very cute puppy that had not quite grown into his body yet. He was just all ears and tail.

"He's cute and kind of dopey!" I initially thought.

Then, I got a bit closer to the door and looked right into the most intelligent eyes I had ever seen. He never made a sound. It was like he had politely knocked and was waiting for an answer.

This was the summer of 2002 and I had just padded into the kitchen around 7:00 a.m. to start the day. We lived on a nice piece of property just south of Tampa, Florida. It was a place made for animals.

Our oldest dog, Chuck, was outside on the porch where the puppy was peeking in. He was our huge Bernese mountain dog who was supposed to be guarding the house. But, well, perhaps Chuck sensed the beauty of it all. Or maybe he was just being a bit lazy.

I called out to my husband, Mike, and told him to come and see what was on the porch. Despite my immediate feelings of compassion, we already had three dogs, two cats, and four horses. Adding another critter to the pack and herd was not really on my "to-do" list at the time.

When we did open the door, Chuck jumped into formation to make it look as if he had been on point the whole time. (Very slick, big boy.) He chased the puppy for a bit down the backyard. Chuck had no intent to harm him; he was just playing guard dog. But, as I said, he was big and looked intimidating. So I worried he would surely scare the puppy. That didn't happen.

The pup just suddenly stopped, turned around, and sat down facing us. I saw courage and kindness in his eyes. And he looked as if he was trying to say something.

"Sorry. Didn't mean to disturb you, but can I come in?"

Chuck stopped. Mike and I stopped. And we all just kind of took in what I learned later would be a very special moment. I had just come face-to-face with a once-in-a-lifetime creature that would not only change my life but also touch the lives of so many humans and dogs in the years to come.

There was a way about him. It was quiet but ran so deep. I also saw a world of cuteness. He was the only dog I ever met that actually had dimples when he smiled. And he had a little lower lip that poked out in such a cute fashion when he looked at me. There was no under bite. It was just part of his adorable face that expressed so many things.

"Look at his little 'doody' lip!" I have no idea why I called it that. It just fit.

This lost puppy eventually became "the one": the dog with the irresistible built-in smile that was sent to me to make a difference. And he completed that journey beyond anything I ever could imagine.

2

Chapter 2

And So It Began

Now, despite being so taken with him, my initial approach on the day he arrived had to be reasonable. The puppy was obviously very friendly and very hungry. He was wearing a dirty, worn-out collar with no name or tags attached. It was really tight on him as well, which led me to believe he'd been on his own for a while and had outgrown it. But he was so sweet, loving, and incredibly well behaved. I could not bring myself to believe that someone would intentionally let him go. He must have gotten lost.

The long stretch of road we lived on had lots of orange groves, acreage, farmers, cows, and horses. It was a busy road at times. Some big trucks came through during rush hour, so we were extremely careful about checking our fence for holes where our dogs could slip out—or another dog could have possibly slipped in.

So on that day, Mike went about the morning ritual, feeding and watering the dogs, cats, horses, and of course the puppy. That was my favorite part of the day. There was so much excitement created when the bowls and buckets came out. The sound of the dogs and kitties happily munching away and the aroma of oats and hay for the horses just floated through the morning air.

In the meantime, I walked the fence line. Inch by inch, I checked everywhere. I found only one puppy-sized hole that our visitor could have possibly squeezed through. And it was really small, even for him.

At that moment, I felt "chosen." Why me? Of all the land and some big homes with plenty of animal-friendly people on a long stretch of road, he'd found me. There must have been a reason.

We went ahead and brought the pup inside to meet the whole family after breakfast. What happened then was pretty much what I expected. The cats hid for a while. Among the dogs there was a lot of sniffing and some territorial growling, but we didn't see any aggression. The pup took it all in. It was almost as if he was prepared for it. He was the only one who never growled or barked. He also didn't cower, or run and hide. He just smiled.

He was black and tan—most likely a shepherd mix with his soft, thick coat. The markings on him were beautiful and perfectly balanced. His eyebrows were more of a golden tan, and they stood out very expressively on his face, which was surrounded by soft and sleek black fur. He smelled like fresh air and sunshine. And when I looked into his eyes again, I saw something so precious. There was a gentle intelligence about him that I had never seen in such a young dog.

There must have been an owner. So, I took off the ratty collar and replaced it with an extra we had. I called the newspaper, local shelters, vets, and everyone else I could think of. It was the right thing to do. Someone must be desperately looking for this puppy.

We heard nothing. So that night, to preserve the peace in the pack, we put the pup out on the porch in a bed with plenty of water and had Chuck sleep out there with him. The weather was nice, and Chuck seemed quite taken with the idea of being the guardian. I tossed and turned a little with worry but eventually got some sleep.

"He made it through the night."

Those were the first words out of Mike's mouth the next morning. The pup had slept peacefully and had good company with Chuck on the porch. As they all ate breakfast, I felt complete but still conflicted about what to do. I had to think about the rest of the family.

Our two younger mixed-breed dogs, Foxie and Guera, were only two years old. They were sisters, and we had brought them into our lives when they were six weeks old. A nice lady we knew had a litter of puppies, and she was giving them away to good homes. They were both very good girls. We had raised them well.

You know how dogs adopt people right back? Well, with littermates, they quite often pick a favorite. Foxie and Mike were kind of a "team." And Guera was the light of my life. She followed me everywhere I went. I loved them both very much. But it was clear who really belonged to whom.

The days of adjustment continued with the pup in the pack as we searched for the owner. Guera was bigger and more of a leader, and Foxie followed. Big ol' Chuck didn't care. The puppy wasn't sleeping on the porch anymore. He was in the bedroom with the rest of us. I crate trained him, of course. That was always a rule with me for any new doggie in the house. He took to it immediately.

More days went by—I'm not sure how many. It really didn't matter. It was clear an owner wasn't going to show up. I refused to drop the puppy at a shelter. Besides, I could no longer continue trying to convince myself that I wasn't in love with him—because I was.

Guera was still my love, and yet the pup fit in with a different kind of love. It was something that seemed like a higher purpose. That would unfold as his life story continued.

CHAPTER 3

IT'S A BOY!

*T*hat was the way I officially announced that the new "baby" would be joining the family. Mike saw it coming, so there was really no resistance. He adored all dogs anyway. We had plenty of space and land for them to play on. So it was obviously time to name the new family member.

Of course, the lady of the household tends to kind of take that on naturally. I wanted something that "fit" his life and ours. Because we were just south of Tampa, I tried to make a connection. I thought of the NFL football team there (the Buccaneers) and considered Buck or Bucky. That didn't fit him. Clancy came up for some reason, but that got thrown out.

Then I reversed and went back to the basics.

"Let's call him Tampa," I said to Mike, as I was making our eggs one morning.

That name seemed to suit him and Mike liked it. So Tampa was officially born again, into our lives.

The next step was to take him for a visit to the vet. After all, I didn't really know anything about his age or health, or if he had even had any of the necessary shots. I was only guessing. He needed the traditional puppy care.

I will never forget that first visit. Tampa rode in my car as if he had been doing it for years. He entered the vet's office walking politely on the leash and immediately wanted to greet everyone—dogs, cats, people; it didn't make a difference to him. He wanted to spread the love.

After his exam and the necessary puppy shots, the vet estimated Tampa's age at around three or four months old.

I thought quietly to myself. "*Seriously? He really is wise well beyond his years.*"

Then the vet said, "He is beautiful and really well behaved. You have done a good job training him."

I responded with the truth. "I haven't done anything. He just came this way."

And so days and then weeks went by. Tampa, Guera, Foxie, Chuck, and the two kitties worked into a nice routine. There wasn't any scrapping or any trouble of that kind. It was mostly playing and watching Tampa just taking in his new life. He wore it well.

He also became quite the comedian as he picked up some new games out in the backyard. It was as if he was there to make me laugh. And it worked every time. Tampa always knew when Mama was watching.

There was a big rope swing in the back part of our property hanging from a huge oak tree. It was there when we moved in. Mike, being a bit of an overgrown kid, would sometimes run out the back door straight to that rope. He would leap up and grab it at the top and swing. "Wooo hoooo!"

After observing this somewhat human behavior for a bit, Tampa decided to give it a try on his own.

I was getting ready to cook dinner one evening and let the dogs out for playtime. The kitchen had a perfect view into the backyard, and this is when I discovered Tampa's new game.

He galloped out the back door that day, sort of mimicking Mike's run, and leapt up with his mouth wide open to grab the top of that huge rope swing. I froze in complete amusement. And then it got better.

He hung on to that rope with his teeth and swung himself back and forth with his back legs and adorable toes all spread out, tail wagging away. His body language was saying "Wooo hoooo!" Tampa was copying Mike's game, and I couldn't stop laughing.

His next adventure was something he created all on his own. And it soon became the morning routine. Our neighbors who connected to the back of our property had lots of cows. I don't know the exact breed; they were just big black cows that gathered along the fence line in the morning to eat.

Well, Mr. Tampa started having a field day with this one. I was once again enjoying watching the dog play from the kitchen window. And it was obvious by Tampa's body language that he had come up with something new. The other dogs were doing the usual sniffing and pooping. Tampa was on a mission.

I watched him creep, hunched down a little, toward the fence where the cows peacefully ate on the other side. They had no idea what was coming—noses were down; mouths were chewing the cud as usual.

When he got about ten feet away, the cows still unaware of his presence, Tampa took off in a direct run right at the fence with a commanding profile and a loud bark. He flushed the "cow covey." Those cows scattered as if a bomb had gone off!

"Eeeeeek!... Moooo!"

Once again, I laughed at my dog comedian until my stomach hurt.

Tampa, being the proud and brilliant animal he was, calmly turned around with a definite smile of victory on his face. He pranced elegantly back toward the house, grinning all the way. The new morning ritual was in place, and he was ready for his breakfast.

The cows never figured this one out—not high on brains, I guess. So, he pulled this trick off almost every morning. I never got tired of watching it. The cows always strolled back in to finish their breakfast, and the neighbors never said a word about it. There was certainly no harm done, and Tampa's humor was something I continued to need, for life began to throw many challenges my way.

CHAPTER 4

DARK TIMES

For a number of months before I even met Tampa, I had begun to feel something dark hanging over me. I wasn't unhappy and nobody was ill. So though I couldn't quite figure out where that feeling was coming from, it was definitely there.

We loved to walk the dogs, ride bareback through the orange groves, grill out, and sit in the hot tub watching the sun go down. We had a nice animal family and a good home. Mike worked full-time as the manager of a fitness center, and I worked mornings for Metro Networks in Tampa, reporting news and traffic for several television and radio stations. That way I could be home the rest of the day to take care of the family. It was a good balance.

Still, I kept feeling I needed to prepare myself for something that I couldn't grasp. It was definitely something very dark, and it came before I was ready for it.

It was October 8, 2002. Tampa had been with us since June or so. He was filling out quickly, as dogs at that age do. And he was becoming even more beautiful every day, with his thick, shiny coat and those deeply intelligent eyes. Everyone had settled in together nicely as a family.

Mike got up early that day, around 6:00 a.m., because the dogs were restless and wanted to go out. I stayed in bed for a bit. I heard the door open and close and smelled the coffee. One of the horses nickered, I think. It was a pretty normal, quiet morning. I had no idea what had just happened.

I just remember Mike bringing Foxie in and putting her back in the bed with me. Tampa and Chuck were also back inside the house, strolling around the kitchen probably trying to get the first "beg of the day" in. But where was Guera?

I couldn't hear Mike anymore, so I sat up in bed and called to him. Then I heard him walking quickly back to the bedroom.

"Guera got hit by a car, but I think she's okay."

I flew out of bed and went running back into the doggie room. He had laid her down right by the door where he carried her in.

"She's not okay," I said.

There was no visible bleeding, but because she was a black dog, it would be difficult to see any at first glance. Her breathing was labored, and her eyes were glazing over. This beautiful creature was badly hurt.

The details of this day are very painful to share, because it is a separate story that I live out in my heart and head all the time. But it is life-changing. And it does all go back to Tampa, and why I believe he showed up in my life that summer.

Because of the early hour and Guera's condition, we had to move fast. Mike carried her to the car, and we headed to the closest emergency clinic, which was at least thirty minutes away. All the other dogs and cats were safely in the house.

That became one of the longest and shortest days of my life. I rode in the back seat with Guera, talking to her constantly as we made our way through rush-hour traffic, trying to get help. She groaned in pain, and I cried, prayed, and begged for her to hang on.

The first two vets who saw her confirmed she had a broken jaw and a dislocated hip. After that, they seemed to be scratching their heads about what else was going on. I started to become very agitated.

"There is something more going on here! Her breathing is labored and her gums are turning white. Can you help my baby or not?" I was sobbing and leaning over Guera, stroking her sweet ears.

They did not have the advanced equipment needed to determine what was happening, and the clock was ticking. So a phone call was made to a specialist in Sarasota, and back in the car we went. It was an hour-long drive. The whole way, as I was gently holding Guera close to me, I kept thinking about the horrific thing that someone had done to my dog.

Mike had found her in the neighbor's yard, lying down with her head sticking up. Whoever had hit her, hit her hard, and they did not even bother to pull over. That is a very sick and twisted part of this story that I just keep burying inside. There were no holes in the fence, so we never figured out how she got to that road.

When we arrived at the clinic, Dr. Heidi scooped her up immediately, noting that her condition was very serious. She found severe internal bleeding from Guera's spleen, and made every effort to stop that while we waited in a private room. We gave her permission to do whatever was needed to save her life. Hours went by. Then the door finally opened, very slowly.

"Her heart stopped." Dr. Heidi teared up as she broke the news.

Mike broke down. I crumpled to the floor sobbing and screaming, "No, no, *no!*"

Dr. Heidi was trying to explain the details, but all I kept hearing was: "Her heart stopped."

And, honestly, I thought mine had stopped, too. It did in a way.

In that very dark moment, only one thing managed to get it beating again: Tampa. I had to get home to Tampa.

Now, make no mistake, the love for Foxie was never forgotten here. When I was able to see through the flood of my tears and my horrible guilt and nightmares, of course I thought of her.

Guera, as I mentioned earlier, was bigger and much more the leader between the two of them. She always looked out for Foxie. So I knew there would be complete confusion there, and many other things that go along with the way a dog mourns. It is more complex than we realize. Watching it is very touching. It's quiet. We can only wonder how much they know.

Foxie stared out the window a lot, looking for Guera, I'm sure. She kept eating and going about life. We took her on a lot of car rides and tried to make things as normal as possible. But I will tell you this: she was never the same dog after Guera was gone. She and Guera used to play fight and snuggle up closely for nap time. Foxie had no interest in any of that with Tampa or Chuck. She just kind of drifted through the days, and I connected with that feeling. None of us were the same after such a loss. Well, almost none of us.

The exception was Tampa. It was during this mourning period I began to realize why he showed up at my back door that summer morning. I obviously had figured out what that dark feeling was looming over me. And as I found myself in the middle of it every hour of every day since Guera's death, there was Tampa. He had come to me for a reason. I was "chosen."

There is no such thing as a replacement for a precious dog that was lost in such a horrific way. That isn't what I am speaking of. I mourned and beat myself up, faked happiness, cried some more, and then tried to laugh. I faced confusion every day.

And during that time, Tampa continued to grow—not just in size, but in maturity, confidence, love, and in the center of my heart. He was my touchstone.

Did he understand the loss of Guera? I'm sure he did. But that was not his focus. His focus was Mama. He was all about me. There continued to be something so deep in those precious eyes. People who met him saw it. Mike saw it. But they didn't see it the exact same way I did. I saw him looking right back at me, and only me. That is the purest form of unconditional love there is. And as we continued to grow up together, that love taught me so many things about myself, and about the direction I wanted to go in my life.

CHAPTER 5

MOVING ON

*I*n 2004, we were hit by some rough times financially, and Mike and I were struggling in our marriage. It was time to downsize on several different levels.

We had four horses we could no longer afford to keep, so I found a huge Girl Scout camp in Central Florida and donated them. It offered four hundred acres for them to live out the rest of their lives filled with love from a lot of young girls. Giving them away was painful for me, but it was the right thing to do for them and for the rest of the family.

I landed a good job as development director at the Suncoast Humane Society in Englewood, which was about an hour and a half from our house. It was a pay increase for me, and we needed the money. But that wasn't the only reason for the career change. The desire to help animals in need was pulling at me, and I'm sure Tampa was responsible for that feeling. The lost pup that found me was now guiding me.

The house and land eventually went up for sale, and we moved into a much smaller house close to my workplace. Shortly after that, the marriage was amicably dissolved, and it was just me, Tampa, Foxie, and my cat, Angel. Mike took along Chuck and his cat, Bear. He adored Foxie, but she had slowly become very attached to Tampa after Guera's death, so he agreed she should stay with me. We were all beginning a new chapter.

Tampa became the man of the house. Now, of course, I still played the role of pack leader. That is very important when you have a home with dogs. His place was to be the man by taking care of me and the rest of the family.

Fear tried to take over many times—and sometimes it did. I was a single woman with three animals in a tiny house, working at a very new job to try to get back on my feet financially. This was one of the times when I really leaned on and learned from Tampa. It was another way he began to save me. He had no fear. There was a spiritual presence within him that made me feel safe.

Even though I worked a lot of hours at the beginning to make ends meet, I was okay with it because I knew he was watching over the household and the family when I wasn't there.

The house was just a few minutes from work, so I always went home for lunch to tend to them. I would grab my purse and head out the door around noon or so.

"I'm going home to let the dogs out!"

This automatically cued the routine chant from some of the staff:

"Who let the dogs out? Woof, woof, woof, woof!"

We were becoming a close family at the shelter, and it didn't take long for Tampa to become a part of it. A few days of the week I would bring him into work with me just to hang out in my office and visit with everyone. It was an environment, however, that Foxie didn't really enjoy. She was timid, so she preferred being home with Angel.

Tampa, on the other hand, loved to go along with Mama anywhere to meet and greet people. It was a job he very much enjoyed. About this time, I started referring to him as "The Mayor." He was always ready to say hello and shake paws with people, and with other dogs.

This was also when I became certain Tampa did have an even higher purpose. I was certainly his main focus. But this wonderful creature obviously had so much to share. The reaction he received from people was remarkable. Their faces just lit up at the sight of him. I wanted to spread more of that around, so I embarked on a mission to try to figure out just how to do that.

CHAPTER 6

SAY HELLO TO CHARLEY

*A*fter Hurricane Charley swept through Punta Gorda and Englewood in August of 2004, leaving so much destruction behind it throughout Southwest Florida, things changed for all of us who rode out that storm. And it put my plans for Tampa and me on hold for a while.

The day Charley was about to make landfall, my executive director called me at home and asked how high my little house was above sea level.

"The latest update is that it is going right over the top of us," she said. "Are you going to be safe there?"

"I don't know," I shakily replied. "It's a rental. I don't know how high we are above sea level, and there are no hurricane shutters."

"Get in your car with your animals and come to the shelter. We are safe here."

So, I put Tampa, Foxie, and Angel in the car, along with a couple of precious belongings that could never be replaced, and we headed out. It was pouring rain already and the wind was whipping madly, but we made it.

I remember calming the animals and watching the eye of Charley going right over us. When a huge oak tree in the shelter's back play yard fell, it sounded like an explosion. But it was a fast-moving storm. It roared in quickly and moved on. Then we had to face what it had left behind.

The shelter was immediately named the emergency shelter for lost animals from all over the area. We were the headquarters, so we temporarily stopped taking in animals that were being surrendered for adoption.

Instead, we spent our time trying to collect pets lost in the storm and reunite them with their families. We also collected pet food and whatever else we could for so many who had simply lost everything.

There were some happy endings, but also some very sad ones. Some people came in every day to see if we had found their beloved pet. The beautiful reunions kept us going, but the empty hearts of so many owners really tore us down inside.

Times like that change a person. My animal family and I were safe. My little house had survived. And I discovered a lot about myself and even more about what I wanted to do from that point forward.

I enjoyed my job of fundraising, writing grants, managing media relations, creating newsletters, planning events... well, the list goes on. But my biggest joy came from the dogs that I interacted with there every day. I would take some breaks during long days to help the volunteers walk them and do some basic socialization and training on them. I felt I had a natural knack for it.

During all of this, Tampa continued to be the light that was always leading me to a new adventure. Once the shelter got back to regular operation after the storm, he started going to work with me again several times a week and went right back to his usual routine of making the rounds. Many people who came in immediately wanted to know if he was up for adoption. No, Mr. Mayor was my boy. But I was proud to let him spread his love around.

He was clearly a master at first impressions. And as I continued to watch him, I finally began to realize what was happening. Tampa was training me! I was following his lead when it came to introducing himself to new dog friends and human friends. He had the perfect, nonintrusive body language that made humans and canines comfortable and responsive. He had the gift of earning respect and love at the same time. The World's Most Perfect Dog had spoken.

CHAPTER 7

THE DOG TRAINER

I parted ways with the shelter in late 2004 because it was time to hunt for the next chapter. I thank God I had Tampa leading the way, or I would have been pretty much lost. I felt like I was putting together a puzzle without having the "end pieces" in the right place. It took me a little while, and I was just living off of savings.

My college degree was in broadcast journalism. Before Mike and I moved to Florida, I had spent over eleven years working in television news. It was a long, fun adventure that I never regretted. But that career will consume your entire life, so as soon as I left it, I knew that world was definitely behind me.

The hunt for something completely different, however, led me in too many different directions. I felt like I was flinging ideas out there as darts and seeing if I could hit the bull's-eye, and nothing was really hitting.

My broadcasting background did finally lead me to a job at Home Shopping Network towards the end of 2005 (almost a year after I left the shelter), where I was hired to work as a guest host selling a food item on-air. Germack Pistachio Company had seen me on a demo reel and decided I was right for their product. They created lovely gourmet mixes of batch roasted nuts and fruits that were very popular. It was a much different way to use my degree, but I liked the people, and I needed the income. HSN was in St. Petersburg, which was just about an hour and a half from home. That was a bit of a hike, but it was not a full-time job so I didn't have to make the drive on a regular basis. Things certainly began to look up financially, but something was still missing.

Then I realized the answer was right in front of me. Tampa. Dogs. The puzzle came together because of him. It was all there in those intelligent eyes of his. It just took me a little time to open my own eyes.

I told you I did enjoy my job at the shelter, but the main reason I did was the dogs themselves. Tampa had led me to that. I wanted more hands-on work with these awesome four-legged creatures. So I tossed out my collection of different résumés and cover letters that just did not fit into my life anymore and followed my heart.

A K-9 boarding/training center just outside the city of Sarasota kept Tampa and Foxie for me once when I had to go out of town on a last-minute trip. It was the only place I could find on short notice, and that turned out to be a stroke of luck. I was intrigued, because they offered not only boarding but also K-9 boot camp training.

This was a program where dog owners dropped off their pets for seven to ten days, longer if necessary, to go through a regimented yet gentle training experience.

I was impressed with the owner's experience, as well as the concept. At that point I was pretty much self-taught when it came to dog training techniques. My parents used to tell stories about how I would "train" our childhood dogs from the time I was six or seven years old. The passion was obviously there from the start with me.

Then I began to think about how much Tampa had taught me about socialization when I took him to my shelter job. I learned to watch his body language and see how he interacted with dogs and people. The simplest things he did every day continued to amaze me. I wanted more. So I decided to make a phone call.

This was a tough one, because I had no formal training working with dogs. Linda was the owner of the K-9 center. And since I had met her, liked her, and boarded my dogs with her, I was really calling for some advice. How do I become a dog trainer?

It turns out my timing was perfect. Linda's assistant boot camp trainer had just resigned. She remembered me, Foxie, and of course, Tampa... so she was willing to set up a meeting to talk. I had no idea where this was going, but I was excited, yet also nervous.

I had no résumé for a job like this. The exception would be my work at the shelter, but I wasn't a dog trainer there. I was writing grants, raising funds, and working on getting media coverage. I just spent time with the dogs when I could. What was my angle here?

Enter "The Mayor." I decided to take him with me. It was going to be a casual meeting outdoors on the property, and Linda was already taken with him. Everyone who had ever met him was, at that point. I figured he could boost my confidence and possibly help me take the step toward this new adventure in my life that I felt was so right. He loved car rides and I needed the company. So off we went.

This was a big turning point for Tampa and me. Linda was more than happy to include him in the meeting. The three of us sat under a huge tree on a park bench by the pond. I don't know how long we talked. It didn't matter. We told stories, hugged on Tampa, and breathed in the outdoors. Dogs that were being boarded there barked and played in the background.

I didn't really even know if it was a job interview or not. That is, until she told me that she would take me on and train me to become her new assistant boot camp trainer! Something just clicked that day. And as Tampa and I rode home together, he had that precious and proud smile on his face the whole way. He knew. In fact, at that point, I believe he knew a lot more than I did about what was coming.

CHAPTER 8

WHAT'S BEHIND DOOR NUMBER ONE?

When I swung the big gate open for my first day of work, I had no idea how many doors would open down the road. The dogs were finishing up breakfast. It was already a very warm day. I wasn't nervous. I just took a deep breath, took it all in, and went to work.

This was where I belonged! No more offices, suits, and sitting in front of the computer for hours. It was outdoors, sunshine and rain, sweat, doggie hair and slobber... and I loved it.

Linda put her trust in me, and I picked up the boot camp training pretty quickly. Working with dogs you always learn something new with each one, so it is a daily adventure that keeps you on your toes.

My job was to train basic obedience: walk nicely on the leash, come when called, sit, down and stay when asked. It may sound simple, but many dogs had their issues. They could be overly shy, or *way* too playful to even focus! I learned to evaluate that and work through those problems to help create happy dogs in loving homes. It was a great feeling to see the reaction from the owners when they came to pick up their pets. I was making a difference.

As this new job experience continued to work so well for me, I did decide to make the move from Englewood to a nice little house in Sarasota to be closer to my dog training and closer to HSN. It cut back a good amount for me on travel time and gas money.

Right around this same time, in early 2007, I had become curious about another adventure going on toward the back of the property at the K-9 center that I was not initially involved in. On Sundays, a group of people would bring their dogs in for protection training. These were the dogs being trained for K-9 police work and in-home protection. Linda had many years of experience working dogs in this capacity, so I started hanging out back there when I was finished with my work. I liked to watch the dogs working with their handlers, going after the decoy wearing the bite sleeve. It was intense and fun.

Now this was not a task for Tampa. He was a lover, not a biter. But it led to something special that I never would have thought of if these folks had not come into my life. And some truly wonderful experiences and memories with my dog were just about to begin.

I was watching the protection training one afternoon, and one of the handlers/trainers who always brought both of his German shepherds in for this started talking about search and rescue (SAR). His name was Mike, and he was certified in SAR. He and Linda had worked with dogs together for some time, and they wanted to see if some of us were interested in putting together a new SAR team.

I should mention, by this time pretty much everyone in this group knew Tampa. We didn't always gather just for training. There were grill-outs and birthday parties, and all properly socialized dogs were invited to relax and have some fun.

We became a doggie training family of sorts, and Tampa was always the beloved life of the party. He would wait politely and "ask" ever so sweetly when the chicken came off the grill, just enough to get a little piece. Then everyone would relax and enjoy the companionship. It all worked.

So when Mike and Linda laid out the plan to get the group together to learn SAR, I was tempted.

"You should bring Tampa!" Mike said.

I wasn't so sure about it at that moment. I mean, you have to envision what I was looking at to understand why.

The dogs they were talking about including were high-priced, pure-bred Dobermans, Belgian Malinois, and German shepherds. These were high-drive canines. They were bred for this.

Don't get me wrong. I knew how intelligent Tampa was. I just didn't know if he really fit into this working dog group. I honestly had never thought about it.

"Oh, come on, Christie. Bring him along! It's all voluntary. Our main goal is to spend more time with our dogs, learn something, and have some fun."

The whole group wanted him in.

So, I figured, "What the heck! Let's give Mr. Mayor a chance!"

A few of the dogs that were joining in had some experience in this. The rest of us were all in the group as SAR rookies. Tampa was the only mutt. God love the mutts! They are full of surprises, and this experience was no exception.

CHAPTER 9

SEARCH AND RESCUE

"Slap some bacon on a biscuit and let's go, we're burning daylight!"
Okay, I borrowed that from the late great John Wayne, but
I don't think he would mind. That is what SAR training felt like at first,
but in a good way. This was the beginning of some very early Sunday
mornings for Mr. Mayor and me. We had to get to work before the hot
temperatures hit.

I quickly learned there are many facets of SAR training. So many, in fact, that I could write another entire book on that subject alone. Weather was always a factor. Mike had a special gauge that would read temperature, humidity, barometric pressure, wind direction and speed. It all affected the dogs and those magical noses they had.

Advanced, certified SAR dogs track and trail through all kinds of weather, terrain, and dangerous circumstances. But, since most of us were beginners, early on we looked for sunny and calm mornings.

Another interesting point is that we did not have one bloodhound on the team. Some SAR teams still accept *only* that breed. The bloodhound's legendary nose is actually accepted as evidence in some courts across the country, in criminal cases. Many SAR experts say they are masters at tracking because their long ears and loose folds of facial skin scoop and trap scent around their noses.

We weren't breed specific, by any means. Each dog that started with our team was unique in his or her own way. That is part of what made it so much fun to watch and experience. As long as they showed us the drive to do the work, we kept on going.

Right off the bat, we learned one of the most important aspects of training a dog for SAR is teaching them the desire to "win." That means they do the job, then get rewarded for it. And this is a very different type of job. It is also important to remember that for a dog, search and rescue is a game. In our world it is certainly very real, and very serious. But to them, it is a game with a fun reward at the end.

There are three basics when it comes to "reward systems" for dog training, which I learned at the K-9 center . There are treats, toys, and then affection—one or any combination of the three could work. The no-brainer with Tampa from the start was affection, especially from Mama. He would do anything for me. I would also learn during this

SAR training that he loved to please a crowd. And I mean, please the crowd to the point where they cheered loudly and applauded him! I'll never forget the first time that happened. But some work had to be done before we got there.

The first phase was footstep tracking. Basically, we had to teach our dogs to put their noses down to pick up human scent. Yes, dogs sniff all the time on their own, but this had to be precise.

We set up the footsteps by digging our heels into the ground and then dragging our feet with each step to help keep our dogs moving forward to follow scent. A treat was dropped in each footstep to encourage and reward, then there was a *big* food or toy reward at the end of that short track. At this point they were tracking their owner's scent and then finding a reward in each step.

You may be thinking, "Well, it sounds kind of like they are putting their noses down just for the treats in each footstep. What good does that do?"

I thought the same thing at first. It felt something like *Hansel and Gretel*: "Follow the breadcrumbs!"

However, during this process, we slowly began to leave fewer treats. There would be one in every two or three footsteps to continue to encourage the dogs. Then eventually all treats were left out, except for the ones at the very end after the dogs had successfully tracked just our footsteps. They were learning to work on human scent alone.

Side to side their noses went, left and right sniffing every single step. That was the precision we were looking for. Sounds simple, but this took some time. Days, weeks, and even a few months went by.

During this time, we also increased the difficulty by making sharp turns and tracks that covered more distance. There was a lot of repetition going on here, and it could be tedious. Step, drag, drop treat...

repeat. We practiced at home during the week, skipping very few days (one or two just to give the dogs a break), and continued to meet every Sunday morning as long as the weather was cooperating. It was time consuming, but we were definitely learning.

I remember one morning I was practicing with Tampa across the street from my house.

A man on a bike pedaled by and asked, "What are you doing there with your dog?"

"I'm training him up for search and rescue."

"Do you mind if I watch while you work?"

"Of course not; he loves an audience!"

So, the man watched, and Tampa and I worked. That actually made it more fun. Tampa got some extra pats on the head, and we had made a new friend. His name was Joe. He was a sweet older man who loved to ride that bike of his, and he would swing by from time to time to watch and ask questions.

"So, Christie, how long before Tampa gets to go out there to find a person? Would he come and find me if I got lost? I get forgetful sometimes."

"Well, I certainly hope so, Joe! That is what we are working towards."

Mike was the one who decided when the teams were ready to move to that next level. And I knew we were all very anxious to really test our dogs.

CHAPTER 10

THE LITTLE MUTT
THAT COULD

*T*his is not to say that Tampa was little, by any means. But he was, as I mentioned earlier, the only mutt on the team. However, that didn't matter. Only heart and drive counted in SAR training.

So, there we were on the big day. None of us beginners really knew what our dogs were going to do. Excitement and nerves were all woven together. We had to remember what we had learned so far.

"Everything sneaks down the leash. Relax and watch your dog. Trust your dog. Go with their instincts."

The important thing on this day was that for the first time, the dogs would be challenged to actually "go find" a lost person. That, of course, would be our decoy who joined us to help out. Tampa would no longer be tracking footsteps that I had made. We were stepping it up to something much more real.

No one was in danger of being "let go" from the team. Remember, it was all about learning and bonding with our dogs. Still, we all wanted to perform at our best.

It was a perfect early Sunday morning for training. There was no rain, and it wasn't too humid. All the teams (eight of us at this point) met at the park at 6:00 a.m. ready to go. For the first thirty minutes or so, it was routine. We walked our dogs for a bit to let them relax and do their business, then we all chatted it up for a little while. Everyone drank their coffee and squinted their eyes at the morning sun, trying to wake up.

After the morning rituals, all the dogs went back into the cars, facing away from the area where the decoy was going to run and hide. Our decoy was Anya, a friend we met at the K-9 center, and she was a great sport about volunteering to come out and help us train up the dogs.

I do want to make it clear that the dogs were quite comfortable in our vehicles. Either the windows were down a bit, or on really hot mornings, we actually kept the cars running for a while to keep cool air flowing. They were relaxing while we were getting ready to put them to work.

Meantime, Mike started by giving Anya a scent article—a marker, a towel, or anything like that. Anya would hold that in her hands and rub it around to get her scent on it. Then she was going to place it in a starting point for the dogs.

Mike then pointed out a route for her to run. It was directly across the open field where we had been doing some short footstep tracking. She was to run all the way to the end, and then turn when she got to the trees to the right, and keep going until she was completely hidden from sight by the full tree line. She also had treats that all the dogs loved as a reward in case they did find her.

Who'd be going first? Tampa. I didn't know why.

Mike just said, "Christie, go get Tampa." Actually, I believe he could see I was getting nervous.

"You don't think he's going to do it, do you?"

"I'm not sure," I said. "I don't know if he is going to understand what I am asking of him."

Mike had a great sense of humor, and he was always full of encouragement.

"Don't worry, just go get your dog."

For tracking like this, Tampa had a harness and a twenty-foot-long tracking lead. That long lead let him get out in front of me and hopefully pull this off. All the dogs had them. I brought him out of the car and gave Anya a chance to love up on him so he could be reminded of her scent. After kisses and hugs, Tampa went back in the car for a bit so he couldn't see where she was going. Anya put the scent article down at the starting point, and she was off and running.

The funny moment here was that Mike had told her to try not to make it too difficult on the dogs. She was supposed to run a straight line to the trees and turn right to hide behind them. But somewhere in the middle, she took a little serpentine path. You know, that thing you're supposed to do when you are being chased by an alligator or something else terrifying?

Mike hollered out, "Anya, back to a straight line!" She gave it the thumbs-up, and we all giggled.

I should tell you that at this beginning point in SAR training, the handlers were supposed to know where the decoy went. That way we could learn to read our dogs and possibly help them a little if they went way off track. So I saw exactly where Anya had done her serpentine move and where she went back to the straight line and made the turn.

After that, we all just waited about ten minutes or so to let the scent settle. Then, out came Tampa. I had to act as if it was no big deal so he could settle. But once that harness and leash were on, it was his cue that it was time to go and play the game.

Mike walked beside me to the starting point, and we pointed out the scent article for Tampa to smell, being careful not to touch it ourselves.

Then I just said, "Where's Anya? Can you go find Anya?"

"Go find" had become my command for him, and that is exactly what he did.

Tampa's nose was right down from the first step, and I felt connected to a brilliant experience. He missed nothing. I had watched Anya's run carefully, and he didn't miss a single step. He even followed her serpentine path when he came to it and then went right back to the straight line. I did nothing but watch him. He had that twenty-foot lead all stretched out in front of me, and I ran along behind him in amazement.

He made the right turn at the trees, nose still down in perfect form, and eventually there was Anya!

"You found me!"

She was as excited as I was. And I was a little bit stunned at what my dog had just done so perfectly. He had no help from me—he didn't need it. He found her all on his own. So, after lots of treats and hugs, the three of us all headed back toward the team home base.

As we came around the trees into clear view, everyone cheered! Mike waved his arms in the air in celebration, everyone clapped, and Mr. Mayor pranced back to his crowd to gather more love and affection. He had that proud smile on his face that I loved so much, and I added my own touch with a few tears. That was a moment.

On that day, no dog on that team did it better than Tampa. In fact, when we got back to the K-9 center, Linda was curious about our morning. She had stayed on the property to work with some protection dogs.

"So, Mike," she said, "who was the best tracker on the team today?"

Mike didn't hesitate.

"I'd have to say Tampa."

"He must be a Doberman, then!" Linda chuckled.

Dobies were always her dog of choice. She had been raising and training them for years, and since I respected her opinion, Tampa and I took that as a compliment.

CHAPTER 11

LET'S GO FIND "HOFFA"

People are so curious about search and rescue. Even I didn't realize that until we started the training. And whether it was among friends or in casual conversations with people I had just met, the same question pretty much always came up first:

"Does your dog find dead people?"

Now I don't mean to show a lack of compassion about something as serious as this, but it was simply their way of asking about what is called cadaver training. And, as you know, that is the search for human remains.

Remember, to a dog, it is all still a game with a reward at the end. So, with that mindset, Mike had come up with a brilliant and rather humorous command to use with our dogs as we entered this phase.

"Go find Hoffa!"

This, of course, referred to Jimmy Hoffa, one of the most famous (or infamous, depending on your view) American figures to disappear inexplicably. Hoffa was president of the Teamsters Union from 1957 until he went to prison in 1967 for attempted bribery, jury tampering, and fraud.

Hoffa was pardoned by President Nixon in 1971 and released. He was known for his long-time involvement in organized crime that began in his early years with the Teamsters, and that connection continued until he vanished in 1975. Hoffa was declared legally dead in 1982. As of this date, his body has never been found.

So the command "Go find Hoffa" definitely had a clever twist to it. Aside from that, this task was also a whole new world of scent for the beginner dogs on the team.

For the first Hoffa day, the setup was pretty simple. We didn't go to the big field where we had been working. This training was introduced on the property at the K-9 center.

Mike brought out a big cinder block, and, as always, our dogs were in the cars so they couldn't peek at what we were doing. It was another early Sunday morning, and I truly had no idea what to expect here.

He then put the "scent" into just one side of the block. A variety of smells came into play with cadaver work: ashes, bones, dried blood, and placenta. These were actual human remains that had been donated to the team. Many people are not aware that you can do that, but in the United States people can donate their remains to help train these dogs to do an important job.

The significant part here is that our dogs had to realize all of these scents were one in the same. They were all Hoffa. What is interesting is that all these scents were contained in such way that we (the humans) couldn't really smell them at all. That would just continue to prove that a dog's nose is thousands of times stronger than a human nose. It was fascinating work, and as much as Tampa and I had learned so far, once again I had no idea how he would react to this.

The beginner handlers did have a chance to watch some of the more experienced dogs work first. We learned they had to give an "indication" eventually with Hoffa. The scent went in one hole of the cinder block, and there was nothing in the other side. The first two dogs went to the block and sniffed on one side, then the other. They inhaled the scent, sat, looked, and barked at their handler. Easy, right?

Many of us were thinking, "Dogs roll around in dead scent all the time, so they will naturally go to that and like it."

Well, that was not necessarily true. Yes, they come back from the yard smelling like something awful, with an odor that is all embedded in their coat and stinks up the house. And they do love it. But that is mostly dead animal stink or poo.

Hoffa was a different kind of stink. Remember that in SAR the dogs have to pick up on a precise scent. And Tampa recognized it pretty quickly. His response, however, was not quite what I expected.

It actually opened up a whole new world of cuteness for him. Being a beginner, I was allowed to help him a little. He was on leash, and I walked him toward the concrete block, giving the command. My instruction from Mike was to have a treat ready, and the minute he stuck his nose into the hole with the smell, reward quickly right at that source.

"Good Hoffa!"

So off we went. Tampa was smiling, as always. He walked to the block, and his nose went in one hole. No reaction. Then he sniffed into the other hole, and *wow*! I didn't even have time to reward. Mr. Mayor went on scent overload. He yanked his head out of there and immediately started drooling, and looking at me with a confused face that I had never seen.

"What in the world was that, Mama? Why did you do that? It stinks!"

His tongue was sticking out, and his bubbly drool got in the way of his treat, so I just praised him and walked him back to the bench to recover. He found Hoffa. He didn't particularly like it. But he found it.

Mike then reassured me that Tampa would likely get over the initial shock of the stink. I wanted my boy to enjoy what he was doing. That was the most important thing. If something continued to put him into drool overload, I figured we would just focus on what he loved, which was finding people.

Eventually, however, Tampa did get past the initial shock of Hoffa. He caught onto that part of SAR pretty quickly, moving on to working off leash and creating his own indication. His was not a bark. He would find, look at me, and then swat at the stink with his paw.

"What's that, Tampa? Did you find Hoffa? Show me, show me!"

And then he would swat at it again. Smart boy.

Hoffa was also getting tougher. By this time, we had pretty much moved away from the concrete block, and began burying the smell under leaves, branches, and sometimes underground. And I mean three to maybe four feet underground. It was amazing.

Tampa's reward system continued to be treats, then the clapping and cheering from the team members. They were pleased to oblige Mr. Mayor, and he was enjoying himself. It was clearly time for the next performance.

CHAPTER 12

NOSE TO THE SKY!

By late 2008, the dogs had moved on to more advanced work on tracking down our decoys and finding Hoffa. The time had come for air-scenting.

Air-scenting also required finding a lost decoy. The difference was that the dogs would not be wearing a harness or the long tracking lead. This was all done off leash. It was geared toward more windy days when tracking from the ground with noses down was difficult, so the dogs learned to pick up the scent by putting their noses up in the air and working with how the breeze was blowing.

"I think Tampa is going to really take to this," Mike said, as we were all gathered in the park in the area where this test was going to get underway.

I had a gut feeling he would as well, because I wouldn't be interfering with him on the leash. That is something I did a lot more often than I intended. My dog was clearly more advanced at this than I was. As usual, he was always training me.

Air-scenting came with a new vest and a little bell we attached to the top of it. When the dogs took off on "the find," the bell would let you know where they were. They were going to run way in front of you, hopefully toward the decoy, and you would run after them. We were going to enter trees and brushy areas where we couldn't see them, so we had to learn to listen for the bell.

Noelle, another member of our team, was the decoy that day. She ran her route through the palmettos and hid behind a tree. Palmettos, if you are not familiar, are small fan-leaved palms native to Florida. There were some narrow paths in between all of them, and that is the route Noelle took as she went to the hiding spot.

"Tampa up first," Mike said.

I didn't feel so much pressure that day, because I had some real confidence in letting him go out on his own. He was just so darn smart. I dressed him up in his new bright orange vest with the little bell attached, and then I walked him out to the starting point. Everyone was watching.

"Okay Christie," Mike said, "tell him what to do and cut him loose."

"Tampa, can you go find Noelle?" I always kneeled down and whispered in his ear. He liked it.

"Go find Noelle!"

Then he was off and running. I was shocked that he didn't weave in and out of the palmettos as Noelle had. He went for the straight route. He wanted to get to her fast, so he leapt over those Florida shrubs, nose up high, tail to the sky with his little bell ringing away.

As for me, I wiped out twice trying to keep up with him, crash-landing face-first into palmettos and heaven knows what else.

"Are you okay, Christie?" Mike hollered.

"I'm good!" I lied.

As I stumbled my way to Noelle's tree, Tampa lapped up treats and love. I had torn a hole in my pants and was picking pieces of palmetto out of my teeth. My dog was simply in the arms of a very welcoming decoy. He had done it again.

CHAPTER 13

GOOGLE DOG

"Is he cheating? He must be cheating. I don't understand how he did that."

This was coming from the rest of the SAR team, of course. It was all said in a joking manner, but they were also scratching their heads about my dog. Tampa did things differently. That is what made him even more perfect in my eyes. The other dogs on the team were pretty much textbook. When they were tracking, finding Hoffa, and air-scenting... it was easy to read them.

Tampa's indications could be extremely subtle—so subtle that sometimes I had a hard time reading him. I was scratching my head at times as well. And no one else on the team had a clue, except for the fact that he had made the find.

To stop any misunderstanding, he had his off days. All the teams did. That is part of the game. But when he was on, it was sometimes hard to believe. And so entered the phrase:

"He must be cheating!"

How in the world does a dog cheat? This conversation came up with a very good friend of mine, Jeff, who worked as the restaurant manager of the Lonjevity Grille in Sarasota. As he poured my wine one night, I talked about SAR training.

We talked about Tampa—the dog that must have scribbled a map to Hoffa on his paw before the test. This was also the dog that must have found a way to go into my purse for some cash, drive to the store, purchase a pair of binoculars, and learn to use them as a device to watch where the decoy was going to hide! The conversation, of course, was getting more amusing as I drank my wine and worked my way through a fire-grilled pizza with extra cheese and hot banana peppers.

I will admit, though, that I got sensitive about things like this. After all, they were talking about my boy. Were they serious?

Jeff had such a wonderful sense of resolve when I became paranoid about such things. We had known each other for a long time, so when he topped off my chardonnay, he had the answer.

"He must be googling! That's it! Tell them he found a little canine computer and he's googling while he's waiting for you to come and get him."

Hysterical! I was the proud owner of "Google Dog." The SAR team actually had a good laugh over this one the next time we met up for training. Tampa loved to make people giggle, and it looked as though he completely embraced his new title. He knew. He was always full of surprises and always the life of the party in so many ways.

We were certified in November of that year in Level 1 Search and Rescue. That meant we had passed the beginner phase of tracking, air-scenting, and cadaver—and we were approved to move on to the much more advanced Level 2. I should add that there was also advanced obedience included here for Tampa, plus some self-defense and pet first aid training for me. Many teams work for years training in SAR before they earn certification for deployment. This was just the first step. But it was exciting!

Most everyone on our team hit that mark together, so we went to our favorite breakfast place to celebrate with oversized omelets and mimosas. Hey, we had worked hard for this. We needed to toast over our morning toast.

Most of the talk that day was centered around the funny stories that brought us to this point.

"Hey, remember training in that big cow pasture? All we could think of was dodging cow pies and hoping the dogs could get past that stink to find Hoffa!"

"Remember when Anya ran to hide and sat down in that big ol' fire ant hill? Google Dog had no problem finding her that day. All he had to do was follow the screams! Eeeeeek!... fire, fire, run for your life!"

Anya made it through okay. Those darn fire ants could ruin a good day, though.

Some of the team members were also starting to talk about what was next for their dogs. They wanted to start with out-of-town seminars and training to keep advancing in SAR.

I had some different things in mind for Tampa. He was first and foremost my partner and best friend. I completed the first phase of SAR training to learn and also to enhance the incredible bond I had with him.

But I wanted to put on the brakes a bit before I took it any further. Deploying a dog on a real-life search can be dangerous. It isn't that I didn't want to get out there and help people. It's just that my boy's safety came first to me, so I started thinking about some other ways I could share his special gift without getting him hurt.

CHAPTER 14

THE NEXT ADVENTURE

*O*f course, I kept on training some with SAR. It was way too much fun to give up, and we had some new team members joining in, so it really became a great social event for all of us. From the beginning, it was all supposed to be about having fun and bonding with our dogs.

Then, a new adventure entered our lives in 2009 that would alter things a bit. And eventually, she ended up altering things in a very positive way. It started with a phone call from my friend Deb. She was the executive director at the Humane Society in Sarasota. Dog people meet dog people. It just happens naturally. The animals bring us together.

On that day, Deb was calling me about a troubled shelter dog named Raja. She had become so stressed out in her environment that she had to be pulled off the adoption floor. Only one or two staff members could really handle her. She was very fearful and attempted to snap at most people who came near her kennel.

To understand Raja's behavior, remember that she was just a younger dog reacting to her life. Her estimated age was about two years, and the staff believed she had been on the street and mistreated as a puppy. Once the shelter got a hold of her, she had been adopted and returned four times, I believe. What was the reason for the returns?

"She needs too much attention."

That is something I always had a big problem hearing. If you want a dog, then be prepared to be the mama or the daddy to that dog. They were created to give attention and love and deserve it back in return. That is what they are here for. If you do not want that kind of love and need for affection or if your life is extremely busy, then perhaps you should rethink bringing a dog into your family.

Getting back to Raja, the shelter had a problem on their hands that wasn't their fault. When a dog develops kennel stress like this, she is pretty much put on the list as "not adoptable." She had never bitten anyone, but she was so fearful she gave the impression that she would if she was pressed too much. She was all fear aggression. Raja needed to get out of there—fast.

Because of the skills I had learned at Linda's and with SAR dogs, Deb asked me to come in and take a look at her, so off I went. This wasn't a job for The Mayor, yet. But it would become one. In the meantime, he stayed at home with Foxie and Angel.

Raja was a beautiful, short-haired, golden-tan mixed breed. It was always a guess. But, looking closely at her, I thought definitely hound (like whippet or greyhound) and some pit bull. She weighed about forty pounds. Her body was muscular and strong, and she had the most beautiful Cleopatra-like eyes I had ever seen. She looked as if she was wearing eyeliner.

The behaviorist brought her out into the meet-and-greet area outside. She had her on a head collar and a short lead. Dogs generally don't love head collars, but given the situation, I could understand why the staff would feel it necessary.

I just relaxed and gave her the opportunity to come to me when she was ready. I could see by her body language that everything she was feeling was based on fear and stress. I said her name and gently dropped my hand down to see if she would approach. She did. She was still on leash, but her tail started to wag and she walked up to me, offering a gentle kiss on the tips of my fingers. I felt an immediate connection.

By this time, you've probably figured out where this was going. I could see the look in Deb's eyes and those of the few other staff members who were there. They were pretty much out of options. They had done everything possible, but Raja wasn't accepting shelter life anymore. Something else had to happen here. There was a good dog in her. I could see it in her eyes. When she collected enough confidence to look right at me, it was as if she was saying:

"Help me, please."

Well, who could resist that? She deserved a chance at a new life. So once upon a time in early 2009, I became a foster mama! Once you start rescuing dogs, it sort of becomes a wonderful habit. Raja needed something different. And I'm not just talking about a new place to live for a while and some training. She needed Tampa.

CHAPTER 15

TIME TO MEET
THE FAMILY

ranted, I made this decision about Raja pretty quickly. A few of
my dog-loving friends thought it may have been too fast, given
that she hadn't met Tampa, Foxie, or Angel at that point, and she did
have some questionable behavior going on.

But I was thinking about Tampa's amazing socialization skills. He
came to me that way as a puppy. And as he grew up and I worked him
through SAR training, those skills became even stronger. I honestly
believe you cannot train a dog to reach his level of dog-to-dog communication. He just had the gift, and I was always the one learning from
him. Now it was Raja's turn to learn from him. Tampa could show her
the ropes in the doggie world.

Raja rode calmly in the car with me on the ride from the shelter to
my house. She stuck her head out the window and let her adorable ears
flap in the wind. She already seemed much more relaxed and really well
behaved. I had to continue to remind myself that I was only fostering

her. The goal was to get her to a point where she could be considered adoptable and then find a permanent family.

The pack accepted Raja very well—Tampa being the concierge, Foxie following in her quiet yet curious manner, and Angel temporarily hiding under the bed. That was normal for them.

Raja, on the other hand, did what was normal for a nervous dog. She christened her new, temporary home with a big ol' poop right in the middle of the living room. Her tail was tucked. She knew it was wrong, and I knew it was never a good idea to scold a dog who was simply reacting to fear. I just put her in the yard for a bit and cleaned up the mess. Poor thing. I was familiar with nervous poops, so it wasn't a surprise. Once she settled that never happened again.

From that point, I let Mr. Mayor do his thing. He was clearly showing his leadership among the pack, and Raja was happily following along. She was pretty rowdy at times, and he took it upon himself to teach her "we don't play ball in the house! Take it outside."

Tampa's calm nature was so contagious it just spread, and Raja was a fast learner. I really liked that in her. The moment she would try to put her paws over Tampa's back, or even hump him (yes, the females do that—it's about dominance), he would whip his head around with a quick, sharp bark to correct her. And she would hit the floor and go into a perfect down-and-stay posture.

I immediately crate trained her. And for the first few nights she went through a "bark fest" in that big crate. The key here is to ignore it. That is tough, because it makes for some nights of very little sleep. However, if you go to tell them to stop or if you coddle them when they bark excessively, then you are giving them attention when they are behaving badly—essentially rewarding bad behavior.

She was a far cry from how easy it was to crate train Tampa. I believe it took him about an hour when he was a puppy! But Raja was a very different dog. Because she was a former street dog, I also had to try to break her habit of wanting to go through the garbage the minute my back was turned.

"Get out of there!" I would say in a firm voice as I was picking up cheese wrappers, foil, and heaven knows what else she had dragged out onto the floor.

She was quite the actress—very skilled at looking sad and tucking her tail. Then she would go right back in there when I wasn't looking. This took some patience and a lot of repetition.

She did have some pretty good basic obedience in her. They had obviously worked with her at the shelter. But after a couple of weeks had gone by, I decided Raja needed more of a "job" to wear her out and help her grow. I thought about some SAR training, but that was something between Tampa and me that was very special. Besides, I thought she was geared more for something else, which eventually turned out to be a whole new world of fun and adventure.

CHAPTER 16

AGILITY!

I have always loved watching dogs run on agility courses. In that competition you see them running at high speed, going through tunnels, tire jumps, and up over hurdles. SAR dogs need some of that training for their work, so a friend from the team had given me a hurdle to work with Tampa on at home. He could run and jump, no doubt, and he had some speed. It wasn't his favorite part of training, but it kept him in good shape.

Raja, on the other hand, seemed like she was built for it. She certainly needed to burn up some energy, so I figured she could watch Tampa run and jump the hurdle a couple of times. Hopefully she would become jealous and excited when he got his treat as a reward, so she would want to try it herself. Dogs do learn from watching other dogs.

"Woo woooo woo, woof, woof, rowrr, woof!"

Can you translate that? I couldn't at the moment. But that was what Raja sounded like when I cut Tampa loose in the backyard to jump over the hurdle. Raja was on the other side of the fence where the yard was divided, and she was going crazy! I mean crazy in a good way, of course. She definitely had some drive for this.

So, I brought her in and started with the hurdle at about two feet. Baiting her with a treat and running along beside her, I said:

"Up, up! Jump!"

She flew over that hurdle as if she had wings on her feet! I continued to raise the height, and within a week she was jumping over three and a half feet.

Either someone had taught her some of this, or she just picked it up from Tampa. Just to clarify, three and a half feet was well over what would be required for a dog her size to compete in an American Kennel Club (AKC) trial. Raja measured twenty-one inches at the withers (top of the shoulders). In competition, she would have to jump only one and three-quarters feet. She was more than doubling that!

Also, her form was amazing. She had what was called great "hind end awareness." She instinctively lifted up her back legs so she would not touch or knock over the hurdle—which would result in a penalty in competition. She was made for this. Most importantly, she absolutely loved it.

Mr. Mayor sat proudly. He took more joy watching her jump than doing it himself. That smile came to his face, and the twinkle in his eye said it all when he looked at me. He was proud of her. He knew what his role was. He was my SAR dog and best friend, always. His new friend had just learned something that would help her in her journey. We were saving her life.

I took the plunge and bought some more agility equipment for both Tampa and Raja. This included a tire jump and two different types of tunnels for them to run through. Foxie and Angel remained my couch babies. They were perfectly happy hanging out watching TV and napping. Tampa and Raja embraced the joy of their jobs.

"Up, up! Jump!"

"Tunnel!"

"Tire!"

Those were the new words entering their vocabulary. Tampa was a four-legged dictionary at this point, because we still had:

"Hoffa! Go find Hoffa!

"Go find Anya! Where did she go?"

It was endless fun. Two dogs with two jobs will keep you busy. Tampa was continuing with SAR. Some of the team members began traveling to seminars for much more intense training. I kept it on the home front, because I just wanted to have fun with my boy. And, of course, the team still enjoyed hanging out at our favorite Sunday breakfast spot for mimosas and omelets after training.

I had, however, always wanted to train up an agility dog because of the excitement of the competition. Raja gave me that wish, in a way. And the whole idea of taking her to the next level was tempting. I worked for a bit with some agility trainers in Sarasota who thought she had great potential. That commitment takes time and money, though, and I had Tampa and the rest of the family to think of.

I also still had my job at HSN and was continuing to train at the K-9 center. If that wasn't enough, something else was about to come my way which would lead to yet another adventure for Mr. Mayor.

CHAPTER 17

SHELTER DOGS AND FOSTER FAILURES

*I*n the spring of 2009 another phone call came in from the Humane Society in Sarasota. Of course, they had called and checked in on Raja regularly. That is a routine thing with a foster dog, and she had been with me for a few months. But the purpose of this call was different.

The behaviorist that had introduced me to Raja was going to be leaving to join a family business. Deb, my executive director friend, knew I had an obvious interest in shelter dogs, and was wondering if I would be interested in taking on that soon-to-be-open position.

This was an easy decision to make. I had learned so much at the K-9 center and made a lot of good friends. But I loved the idea of taking those skills and using them to help abused, troubled, and stray dogs find forever homes.

Linda supported my choice. She knew me pretty well by now and probably figured I would eventually choose this route. Also, the shelter was a good bit closer to home. So I gave proper notice and made the move back into the animal rescue world, this time as a behaviorist. Deb was flexible with my hours because I definitely wanted to keep my gig at HSN. It was going well.

My job description at the shelter was similar to what I was doing with Raja. I was to evaluate the dogs, pinpoint any problems, and work on their obedience and socialization. The other task was to find ways to keep their stress levels down so they didn't start reacting to kennel life in a negative way. That could include things like giving them lots of human interaction or finding a compatible doggie friend at the shelter for them to play with. As it turns out, for some the answer was agility. The shelter had a pretty nice course set up in one of the yards. That was a positive way for very active dogs to burn up energy.

Raja and Tampa didn't get neglected due to my new job. They both kept their K-9 jobs. Raja's self-esteem was growing through agility, and Tampa was still enjoying SAR. Several people at the shelter already knew him, and of course they knew Raja. I didn't take her in to visit because that would almost definitely frighten her, but Mr. Mayor came along with me from time to time when we had fundraising events. It was all about the people for him. He never stopped loving it.

Meantime, I was becoming rather attached to Raja. We had definitely connected, and I was also worried about her future. My job as a foster parent was to tame that fear in her, teach her some obedience and manners with other dogs and people, and then see if we could find a permanent home for her. She had come such a long way, and the agility was a real bonus for both of us.

I remember looking out the window into the yard one morning, watching her trotting around chasing lizards. Her floppy little ears were bouncing up and down, and she would look through the window at me from time to time with those Cleopatra-like eyes just to check in. She was so darn cute. I kept saying to myself, really speaking to her,

"Don't worry, baby. I'm not going to let anything happen to you."

I tried, but I couldn't picture her in any other environment. She had Tampa as her teacher, and she clearly loved me. The other two kids had accepted her as long as she didn't try to steal their spot on the couch, eat their food, or change the channel on the TV.

There was really only one logical conclusion. Raja was already home. When the reality of that hit me, I was elated. I knew I was making the right choice.

So, on July 18, 2009, after I had been working dogs at the shelter for several hours, I took a break and went inside to talk to Kerry. She was in charge of adoptions and fosters. When I sat down, she smiled at me with a knowing look.

"What's up, Christie?"

"I'm keeping her." I said.

Several others heard it, and a round of applause went off! They were all praying I would make that choice because things were going well for Raja, the formerly struggling dog who deserved a good life.

"Ladies and gentlemen, introducing Christie, the foster failure!"

I felt proud to carry that title. It happens to a lot of foster parents, so I was in good company.

Raja Fletcher officially became a part of the family that day. Looking back, it's hard to believe we were only halfway through the year. Some wonderful things were coming together. And it was only the beginning. The next adventure was all about Mr. Mayor.

CHAPTER 18

PET THERAPY

Shortly after I adopted Raja, the SAR team moved training from Sarasota to Englewood, in an area that was about an hour away. There was more open space there. Tampa and I continued some training with them, but that was a bit of a hike, and I had the rest of the family and two jobs to think about. Also, they were moving to the advanced training level that I spoke of earlier, and I was still certain I didn't want to take my boy quite that far.

Everyone who worked at the shelter had gotten to know Mr. Mayor. And one person in particular had something very special in mind for him. Kate was in charge of pet therapy.

Of course, I knew immediately Tampa was perfect for it, given his overwhelming compassion for people.

Still, I put my poker face on just for fun and rubbed my chin a little.

"Kate, I just don't know if Tampa is geared for that."

At that moment she walked toward me, raised her sweet little eyebrow, and threw a box of Milk Bones at my head.

71

No, seriously, she knew I was kidding around. I was excited about getting Tampa involved with this. Kate certainly had faith in him. And it was such a wonderful thought to share all his love with people in nursing homes and assisted living communities.

The training for this is more complex than you may think. It isn't just taking a well-mannered dog and walking him into one of these facilities. The special canines that do this must be able to tolerate a lot of different smells and people who are dealing with different types of ailments as well as having different emotions.

I had no fear when it came to Tampa facing this new challenge. I knew he would blow through the training without a hiccup because that is who he was. Once again, his desire to give love just overcame any element of doubt or fear in him.

"Pull my ears, touch my toes, scratch my head, make loud noises, and tug on my tail. It doesn't bother me a bit!"

Mr. Mayor might as well have been saying that during his training sessions. He always looked to me for approval, with that great big warm smile of his.

"Good boy, Tampa," I would say.

That is all he needed. We had to put him through this routine because the folks he would be visiting would very likely do all these things. He was also introduced to wheelchairs, walkers, and anything else that he might encounter. Nothing phased this dog. And believe me, a great number of other dogs are frightened by things like that. It just looks too odd to them. Tampa easily took it all in. It was the way he approached life.

This turned into another adventure where Tampa was actually training me. He walked right up to those wheelchairs. He slid his head up under the walkers and worked carefully around the canes because he wanted to make the gentle approach to greet the person. I did not teach him this. He already knew how.

"Will he get up into a chair and sit down, so he can be higher up and closer to someone?" Kate asked, as we were training at the shelter one afternoon.

"Sure, I guess." I looked at Tampa and lightly patted the seat of the chair.

"Up, up, chair!" This was a newer command for him.

And up he went, grinning all the way. He sat in that chair just as if he belonged there and let the volunteer who was helping us rub his ears and his whole face. It may not sound like a big deal, getting up in a chair, but it is important that a therapy dog does this properly and sits still, making no sudden movements and not wiggling around. Otherwise, he might scare someone. Tampa weighed around fifty-five pounds, so his size had to be considered. The goal was to make people comfortable with him.

Truth be told, this training was a formality for Tampa. He had to go through the process, but Kate and I both knew he would easily pass all the tests and earn his certification. And he did. In the early fall of 2009, we were a certified pet therapy team. Mr. Mayor looked dapper and proud in his brand-new red pet therapy vest, with his certification patch.

"Ask to pet me; I'm friendly," is what it read.

It was time for him to spread the joy.

CHAPTER 19

MAKING NEW FRIENDS

$\mathcal{S}$o many thoughts were running through my head as the sliding door at the nursing home opened and we felt the nice cool air hit us. It was so quiet. The feel of it was a far cry from running through fields listening for Tampa's little bell, watching him leap over palmettos, and hearing the cheers of our SAR team.

But that was the beauty of it. Tampa's versatility really came out here. At first, one of the employees at this facility went with us for visits.

However, when she saw how well Tampa and I handled it, we were off on our own.

He tiptoed down the hallway, as if he had been doing this his whole life. He wasn't afraid. There were people resting that we didn't want to wake up, so we both padded around quietly, peeking inside open doors to see if anyone wanted a visitor.

"Miss Rose? Would you like to say hello to the doggie?"

She was an adorable little lady sitting in her chair watching some TV. I'd never met her, of course. I just read her name at the entrance of her room, and I always believed it was sweeter to call them by their first name, with the preface of Mr. or Miss.

She peeked through her glasses.

"Oh! Look at the puppy. Hi puppy!"

That was Tampa's cue. He gave me the look, and I gave him the nod and wink. We had created such a bond at this point that was all it took.

Miss Rose had a walker in front of her chair. She opened her sweet little hands to welcome Tampa, and he slid under that walker to rest his chin gently on her leg. She laughed and petted his head.

Actually, I should say, she "patted" his head. Pat, pat, pat! It was almost as if she was swatting him. That's just the way her little hands worked, and this is where the training came in. Obviously, this wasn't the traditional way of touching and petting a dog. I watched Mr. Mayor very closely just to be sure he was comfortable.

"It's okay, Mama, she's giving me love."

He spoke with his eyes and his smile, and everything was very much okay. He didn't pull back or try to duck away. Miss Rose's affection was completely understood and embraced by him. I believe he made her day.

After several visits to this same nursing home, Tampa and I were pretty much in a routine. We had our regulars, and some new friends would arrive from time to time. One person in particular was pretty memorable.

Miss Doris did not like dogs. The staff politely told me this from day one. Tampa and I understood, so we were careful to stay out of her room and work around her when she was watching TV with a group.

Surprise! Mistakes do happen. I was rounding a corner hallway with Tampa one morning, and a nurse was rolling Miss Doris in her wheelchair around the same corner. None of us knew we were all headed right for each other.

Bonk! Miss Doris's fist came down right on top of Tampa's head. She didn't say a word. She just clocked him. I quickly moved him to my other side away from her.

"Remember the training, Christie," I spoke to myself.

Everything was good, as everyone stayed calm. The nurse and I shared knowing glances, and we rolled on in the opposite direction. Tampa's look at that moment was almost as if he was giggling. He sparkled in his amusement, and we eased along to say hello to some more of our friends.

Miss Doris wasn't strong enough to hurt him. I was just worried she might have dented his dignity. Not on your life! That's just not how he rolled. It made me wish I could take a bonk in the head and recover that quickly. I'm willing to bet most of us have felt that very same way at some point in life.

So we pressed on having some fun, and in the early summer of 2010, Tampa and I had the chance to mix things up a bit. There was a summer camp for kids in Sarasota, and they had asked Kate if she could send over some therapy dogs to visit. It was too hot outside to play, and the children needed some fun things to do.

Now, bear in mind, even some very experienced therapy dogs would not respond well to a swarm of kids who all wanted to pet and touch them at the same time. It was a completely different feel than a nursing home. Mr. Mayor did not mind. In fact, he was having a blast! There were lots of questions about dogs in general and about SAR, and the hugs just kept coming.

"What kind of dog is he?"

"Does he really find people who get lost?"

"Oh, he just licked my nose! Heehee!"

Their curious young minds were so much fun. We had a wonderful day. And as it turned out, this special experience also kind of turned into a "send-off" from my perspective. Changes were on the way again.

CHAPTER 20

ON THE ROAD TO THE Q

Tampa consistently brought positive energy my way. And I needed that greatly, because life was always throwing me unexpected challenges. We all need a support system. Sometimes that comes from people. Sometimes, it's from a special companion with four legs and a fluffy tail. As you have gotten to know him, I'm sure you can see he was always ready for a new adventure. This next one was very big for the whole family.

It was July of 2010. My kitty, Angel, had gotten sick. Well, she *was* old. She was also one that had found me many years before the doggies came into my life. Someone had dumped her in my apartment complex when I was living in Texas. She followed me up the stairs and just walked right through the door with me when I got home from work one day.

Angel never showed me any signs of suffering in her old age, but she had been slowing down for quite a while and spent most of her time in her favorite little bed. Then, one night, my little blue-eyed child faded away peacefully in her sleep. Even though it wasn't unexpected, it still really hurt. But it was her time, and as her angel wings spread, the upcoming change made more and more sense.

Germack Pistachio Company, the one I worked for on-air at HSN, had decided to make the move to QVC. They had no intention of going without me, and I was completely on board because it was a very positive move. It's just that I had to work out the logistics of the whole thing. I lived in Florida, and QVC is in Pennsylvania. The president of Germack flew me back and forth a number of times to go on the air at the Q, but that was expensive, and I didn't know how much longer he would be willing to do that. He was loyal to me, but he had to think about the company. And I had to think about all the possibilities.

"Load up the moving truck; let's take a one-way road trip!" I was talking out loud to myself again. It's how I worked things out.

I could be a little crazy impulsive at times, but my thought process here was actually pretty simple. I loved my job as the behaviorist at the Humane Society, and I planned on continuing my work with shelter dogs in the future. But the job from Germack was the one that paid most of the bills, and QVC was growing our brand pretty quickly. You have to go where you can make the best living.

Over the years I had learned a lot from Mr. Mayor. And this knowledge really came into play here. He was fearless, passionate, and ready to take on anything new at a moment's notice, smiling all the way! I looked into his eyes as the rest of the family was already asleep late one night. He always stayed up with me.

"Tampa, we're going. And you are riding shotgun."

He cocked his head and gave me that smile and his happy pant with that little pink tongue sticking out. Then we both drifted off to sleep on the couch. We were ready.

Yes, I rented a twenty-two-foot moving truck. I had a trailer on the back pulling my SUV, and I drove it all by myself with three dogs by my side. Sure, I was scared. But once I hit the road and got comfy in that huge vehicle, I started focusing on the life ahead of us.

"Jesus, take the wheel."

Thank you, Carrie Underwood, for that powerful song, because it was rolling over and over in my head as we crossed many state lines while heading for our new home.

I had found a really nice rental house in Lancaster during one of my trips when I was going on-air at the Q. It was a small red brick house at the top of a hill in a quiet neighborhood. It backed up to a woodsy area and had a big fenced-in yard, which was perfect for the dogs and me.

I chose Lancaster because there was so much beautiful countryside, and it was a very animal-friendly area. There were horses, dogs, cats, and lots of wildlife to embrace.

So many thoughts were running through my head as Florida slowly drifted away from us. After all, this was a big move.

Fortunately, it was a good "thinking" drive. You know how human babies fall asleep easily if you drive them around in a car? Well, this big truck worked the same way with my dogs. Tampa, Raja, and Foxie pretty much crashed during most of the drive. They woke up at the rest stops to pee and poo. We also had three hotel stays to sleep and "reboot."

I took those down times to keep my friends in Florida, and around the country, up to speed on how the trip was going—posting pictures on Facebook as I crossed state lines. That helped keep me going. They loved to see me driving that big ol' truck!

"You ARE my truck-driving mama hero!" That came from Julie, a long-time high school buddy.

Horseback riding friend Kathy Jo wrote: "Seriously.... did you drive that truck from Florida to PA all by yourself?"

Yes, I surely did. And then, over one thousand miles after leaving the original launch pad, we were home. In early September of 2010, we said hello to Lancaster, Pennsylvania.

CHAPTER 21

TAMPA TO THE RESCUE—AGAIN

Our house was only about an hour or so away from the QVC studios in West Chester. That was very reasonable to me, because I was not going to be driving into work every day. Germack was doing well, but technically we were still being introduced to QVC's customers, so my on-air appearances were a bit scattered and my hours were odd. I could feel the momentum building, though. It was exciting!

In the meantime, once we were settled in at the house, I knew it was time for Mr. Mayor to go back to work. Foxie found comfort on a new little bed I'd bought her. I had brought my agility equipment along for Raja, and that was all set up for her in the yard. Tampa still ran on the course some, but there were people out there who needed to meet him.

The nursing home that was just fifteen minutes from my house was our first stop. I called ahead, and we set up a visit to get Tampa signed up for pet therapy. That was easy. We were right back into our routine.

There was, however, a new situation created by the ever-so-adventurous Raja that would call for Mr. Mayor's patience and brilliance.

This goes on the record as a major Christie "duh" moment. Yes, my yard was surrounded with a nice wooden fence, but it wasn't as high as the fence in Sarasota. Raja's jumping skills had gotten stronger.

So, as we were all hanging out on the patio one late summer afternoon, she did exactly what I'd taught her to do—she jumped. Only this time it was up and over the backyard fence, and off she went.

I had the perfect, calm and assertive certified K-9 trainer reaction. I panicked! My fear was that we hadn't lived there that long, and she would possibly lose her way. Raja was very pack-oriented at this point. She wasn't trying to run away from home, but there were bunnies and all kinds of other critters she wanted to chase, and that instinct just took over.

I tried everything you are likely thinking of right now:

I drove the car around: "Car ride, Raja... come get in for car ride."

No dice. Oh, she saw me. She was circling the neighborhood, and she would stop, and look right at me.

"No way, Mama; I'm havin' a blast!" And off she ran again.

I then drove back to the house and tapped on her food dish loudly with a metal spoon. It was like ringing the dinner bell.

"Yum yum times! Come get your yum yums, Raja!"

She was laughing at me—darn dog. She was having a blast laughing at me while I was having a panic attack. She would look at me out of the corner of her eye, come close to the house, then dart away again with a triumphant look on her face. She continued to circle.

"This isn't funny, Raja!"

I took a deep breath and put Foxie inside, then Tampa and I sat on the patio to try to think of something else. Of course, that "something else" was sitting right there looking deeply into my eyes, giving me that comforting smile. And I was about to witness something amazing.

"Tampa, can you go find Raja?"

Mr. Mayor was on the move—no leash, no nothing. I knew he wouldn't go on the run away from Mama. It did take him a couple of minutes to wrap his head around it. SAR dogs were trained to "go find" humans, not animals. But this wasn't just any animal—this was family. Raja was clearly playing a game with me. Perhaps she would listen to him.

He circled my car for a minute because, as I told you, she had come close to the top of the driveway and then took off. He was beginning to pick up scent. I had Raja's leash in my hand and repeated the command to him.

Then I glanced far down the hill. She was standing there, *way* too close to the main road that connected to our quiet little street. I was trained to stay calm but was honestly scared to death. I looked at Tampa, and he was looking right at her. I didn't move, because I knew she was still toying with me and would dart off again. She was now less than ten feet from that busy road during rush hour. The memory of what had happened to Guera had me frozen in fear.

I looked at him. "Tampa, can you go get Raja? Please go tell Raja to come home."

I held my breath. He began to trot very casually, directly toward her down the hill. She stood still, looking straight at him. It was so quiet, and what felt like forever really only took minutes.

Mr. Mayor got to her. He went nose to nose with her, obviously "saying" something, and she went right into a perfect down and stay. She didn't move. Then he looked at me.

"Come on, Mama. I've got her."

I breathed, and walked slowly down the hill to her. Tampa was still standing over her as she stayed there calmly and let me put the leash on her. The three of us walked quietly up the hill and safely back into our little home.

I was stunned yet proud and wished I had a camera to capture this moment. It was an amazing display of perfect dog-to-dog communication. They *do* speak to one another. We know that. I have no clue what he said to her, but it didn't matter. Raja was safe. Another job was spectacularly pulled off by The World's Most Perfect Dog.

And make no mistake, after that I rigged something in the yard especially for Raja to make sure she didn't ever go on a fence-jumping adventure again.

CHAPTER 22

SHELTER DOGS IN NEED

*T*ampa and I knew it was coming. It is all about timing. I was busy at the Q, and we continued to adore our pet therapy work, but that special place in my heart for shelter dogs was always going to be there.

I had done some poking around right after we settled into the move to Lancaster, looking at rescues and shelters. I chose one in particular that was close enough to home, and the president, Joan, had happily invited me in for a meeting at the Humane League of Lancaster County. This was late in the fall of 2010. There were no positions available at the time, but she appreciated my passion and my background with shelter dogs. And, well, after a little storytelling on the phone (as doggie people do), I truly believe she really wanted to meet Mr. Mayor.

Joan, Tampa, and I had fun getting to know each other. She gave me a tour of the shelter, and that powerful love and compassion for these dogs came flowing back as I saw those big eyes and sweet faces looking back at me through their kennels. I wanted to help. And my gut told me the right time would come for Tampa and me to do that.

In the summer of 2011, the phone call came in. Joan's behaviorist at the Humane League had moved on, and she wanted me to join the team. It turned out this job carried even more responsibilities than my job at the shelter in Sarasota. I was going to be the head of BARC, the Behavioral Assistance and Rehabilitation Club. This meant that not only would I be working with shelter dogs, but I would also be putting volunteers through the BARC training program to teach them how to connect with these dogs. The goal was to help the dogs deal with kennel stress, or any other issues, so they would become more adoptable.

The beauty of this was that it would bring yet another opportunity for Mr. Mayor to work his magic. He already had quite the résumé with SAR and pet therapy. To add to all that, remember how I let him train Raja when she first came home? She was one troubled girl, and he changed her life, so I wanted to work him into the BARC program with me to help the volunteers and the dogs. Joan thought it was a great idea.

So, once again, Tampa and I were on the move. We were determined to continue our mission. The lost puppy that had been dumped on the side of the road and found me was ready to go to work with shelter dogs that needed his help.

Joan allowed me to make some adjustments to BARC. And as we got started, I realized the real potential of this training program. We had some very dedicated volunteers: some older, some younger, some working or going to school, and some retired. They were dog lovers from all walks of life. I split them up into teams of eight or fewer, because that was a manageable number, and they all got to meet Mr. Mayor during their first session. He was going to be my partner, after all. They loved the idea. He was as much of a trainer as I was. Actually, he was the smarter of the two of us, as you well know.

Oh, the fun we had from day one! We were dedicated, no matter what we faced on a daily basis. Pennsylvania is full of weather year-round, but we showed up no matter what—ready to sweat, or bundled up for cold, wind, snow, and rain.

"The wind is going to be a factor today!" I said several times.

"What did ya say? I can't hear you. I think my ears are frozen!"

"*Ouch*! I just wiped out on a patch of ice!" That was me, the wipeout queen. Ice was not my friend.

It's tough to work with dogs when toys and agility equipment are bouncing and rolling around as if they have a life of their own, and all you can hear is the whir of wind in your ears. And the feel of ice under your feet is never good.

Sometimes we were forced to work indoors in a training room, but we pressed on with outdoor sessions as much as possible, as long as it was deemed safe enough for us and for the dogs. It was important for them to get out into the yards to play, learn, and socialize.

By now you know who the "socialization king" was. After the first few rounds of BARC training with just me, the volunteers, and the shelter dogs—it was time to take things to the next level.

CHAPTER 23

BRINGING IN THE MAYOR

*T*he volunteer teams had already met him, as I told you. But on that day, it was just to say "hello." I wanted to get better acquainted with them one-on-one, as well as with the dogs we were focusing on before Tampa really came into the picture to go to work. It was all a process.

During the first real training session with Mr. Mayor, I had him off leash with no fancy tricks or collars. It was just Tampa and me. We were not trying to show off. That was not the point. The point was for them to see what this formerly neglected, abandoned dog had learned over the years. His focus and calmness was amazing to watch.

Now, I did not expect such advanced obedience to happen with these shelter dogs. Tampa and I had worked a long time to reach that point. What I wanted was to give the volunteers some hope and excitement. They were playing a major role in securing these canines a forever home by learning how to teach them some basic obedience and focus. BARC was meant to be much more than just taking the dogs out for exercise and ball play. The dogs had to walk nicely on a leash, take treats gently, and refrain from jumping on people—all the things that made them good, adoptable dogs.

The volunteers were really learning, and their enthusiasm did, indeed, begin to sneak down the leash. Our project dogs were coming out of their shells and learning some nice manners. My revised BARC program, with Tampa by my side, was making things happen.

In fact, Mr. Mayor had become such a positive influence at the shelter the staff asked if they could include him in something a bit more challenging.

As I'm sure you know, shelter dogs must be evaluated when they first come in. That meant mostly looking for medical issues, plus getting a read on temperament and personality: Were they shy or hyper? Did they act terrified or show aggression toward people and other dogs? The full-time staff took care of that when the dogs were dropped off.

The aggression was the most difficult to pin down with questionable dogs. If it was showing up, we had to figure out its true cause. It could have been true aggression or possibly fear and stress, just like Raja. Shelter life can bring out things in some dogs that were never present before. Let's face it, their lives had been turned upside down.

Dogs that were aggressive toward people were easier to pinpoint. Possible dog-to-dog aggression was more difficult to spot, because they could have been just trying to communicate something and not necessarily wanting to start a fight.

Enter The Mayor. He was a master at reading other dogs, and I was well trained at reading his body language. Becki, the shelter manager, had observed that. And she needed our help.

Here is how it played out: There were certain dogs that were not on the adoption floor yet because they would growl and snarl when other dogs were walked past their kennels. Remember, many of them were strays, so we didn't always have a lot of background on them. But it was unfair to judge how they acted inside their own space. They needed to be tested with another dog out in the big play yard to get the full picture. That other dog became Tampa.

I will remind you again, I would have *never* put my boy in danger. Every precaution was taken to make sure he was not suddenly attacked by a shelter dog. Becki was always there holding the shelter dog tightly on leash. I had a good hold on Tampa, and out into the big yard we would go.

We had interesting experiences. Tampa would easily let me know if things were okay by approaching and showing me he was comfortable with certain dogs. Most were just playing too rough or simply didn't know how to act around another dog. He did some teaching. A nice handful of these dogs improved and eventually the "dog-aggressive" note on their record could be removed.

One in particular, though, was a completely different animal. And even after working with a number of aggressive dogs in my training career, this was a new one for me.

Her name was Ginger. She was a beautiful blue/gray pit bull, and she *loved* people. She gave tons of hugs and kisses during training, but she was not on the adoption floor yet because the staff told me she was showing consistent signs of aggression toward other dogs. It was time for a true test.

Tampa and I went into the big yard first, then Becki came in with Ginger. She moved slowly. Both dogs looked at each other, held tightly on leash. I didn't see anything alarming, and neither did Tampa, or he would have backed up. I gave the usual meet-and-greet command.

"Make friends! Let's make good friends!" I spoke in a nice, sweet tone.

Ginger went into a perfect down, with a relaxed look on her face. Becki still had a tight hold on her. I walked Tampa up closer to her, and he didn't resist. He reached out his nose to sniff from about five feet away, then came the shocker.

Ginger's eyes turned black, and she *launched* at him—snarling with her mouth wide open. It looked like a shark attack. Tampa and I immediately jumped backward, and Becki pulled Ginger away. They made no physical contact whatsoever, not even close. No one was hurt.

I circled Tampa, and he sat down, refusing to even look at Ginger. I patted his head and looked at Becki. She looked at me. No words needed to be said.

I believed someone had actually trained Ginger to do this, because dogs don't normally go into a perfect, calm down with soft eyes and then launch like that. She gave no warning whatsoever. We had a problem here.

The final word on Ginger was that she definitely needed to be the only dog in the household. That makes for a tough adoption, so her future was shaky. For the record, I didn't make final decisions about such things. I just shared my experiences with the dogs. As I recall, Ginger ended up at a special rescue where she was separated from all other dogs. This was a place that would keep dogs and care for them indefinitely if they could not find a forever home. I always prayed Ginger somehow found her way to an owner that could handle her, though. She so loved people.

CHAPTER 24

TAMPA AND LOGAN

There is one thing that is inevitable when you work with shelter dogs. Naturally, you grow to care for all of them and help in every way possible to find them a forever home. But there is always one that grabs your heart. It happened at every shelter I worked with.

In Lancaster, it was Logan. We met in early 2013, and there was an instant connection. He was a beautiful reddish-brown-and-white pit bull, who looked a touch like Petey from *The Little Rascals* (without the patch around his eye). He had such a sweet face, and he loved to lean up against people, give lots of hugs, and flop over on his back for belly rubs. There was, however, one problem.

Logan did not take to shelter life very well. It wasn't the staff or the volunteers. It was some of the other dogs—mostly the hyper, barky males. They agitated him to the point where he gave the impression of a dog that might attack another dog if he had the chance.

Now, remember, I wasn't involved in the initial evaluation when they first came in because I wasn't a full-time employee. Also, I was getting busier at QVC, so I had to spread out my BARC training days a bit more. Joan was very understanding about that, because we were still making great progress.

My point is that when I was introduced to Logan and looked at the card on his kennel, I saw there was an issue: "Does not like other dogs, especially males." That is not a good thing. He was not on the adoption floor because of that. So it was up to BARC to try to get him there.

As a dog trainer, I would never claim to be perfect. Tampa and I were initially fooled by Ginger. It happens. But in Logan's case it was different. I just wasn't buying it.

I kept looking at that card. "Does not like other male dogs."

This animal had been misdiagnosed. I could just see it in his eyes. He only got agitated at a couple of male dogs we had to walk him past to get out to the big yard. And those two boys were barkers! Logan wasn't aggressive. He was upset. He was playing defense. I could feel it in my gut. So, what do we do now?

"Tampa, I need your help."

I had to prove something to put this dog in a better position so he could find a home. Mr. Mayor was my only hope. The BARC teams agreed, and Joan and Becki gave me the go-ahead. The plan was set.

The first thing we did was move him to a quiet kennel, isolated from other dogs. Trust me, this was not a cruel thing to do with a dog like Logan. He immediately showed signs of relaxing because he was away from all of the kennel barking. He was never ignored. We all spent a lot of time playing games with him and taking him out.

Then it was Tampa's turn, and I must tell you ahead of time, this was a beautiful thing to watch. We worked on leash first, of course. Tampa took to Logan right away, never showing me signs that he felt any aggression. He approached Logan in a calm, assured manner. And then he played "teacher," much as he did when I first brought Raja home. Things were going just as I had hoped. After just a couple of sessions, it was time to take the leashes off. I was that confident all was fine between these two.

We were working in the quiet yard just behind the vet clinic at the shelter. Logan was already out there, and I walked Tampa past one of the vet techs who was sitting outside.

"Ahhhh, be careful. Logan does not like other dogs." She said this with a rather tense look on her face.

"Don't worry," I said. "That isn't quite true. He loves Tampa."

The yard gate was closed, leashes came off, and away they went. Logan wanted to play! He just needed to learn how. He was young, so he also wanted to test Mr. Mayor by putting his paws up over his back. That is what doggies do. Tampa corrected, and Logan accepted by flopping over on his back.

I had two BARC trainees with me, watching the whole thing. Tampa was confident, rewarding Logan with kisses when appropriate and correcting him when needed. Dogs growl when they correct. That is how they communicate. It just has to be the right kind of growl, like a parent correcting a child. It's not cruel, but simply firm enough to get the point across. And he was wagging his tail the whole time. He loved teaching his new protégé.

"Good boy, Tampa!" I continued to encourage.

Logan got the zoomies, as young dogs do. He went flying around the yard running circles around Tampa, then slamming on the brakes right at him with his overzealous play.

"Grrrr, rowrrrr... Woof woof!" came from Tampa as he whipped his head around to stop that behavior.

"Oh no... here it goes," came from one of the volunteers. Clearly it made her nervous.

"Let him do it," I said. "He's doing his job."

There was, of course, no biting. Logan would immediately flop over on his back when he was corrected, smiling in complete submission. Then Tampa would prance up to me with that happy face, tail up and wagging.

"How's that, Mama?!"

Another job well done by Mr. Mayor. The staff was eventually convinced that Logan was not aggressive. He enjoyed the quiet, private kennel he was kept in, and Tampa and I visited and played with him often. But Logan couldn't get adopted that way because he couldn't tolerate the adoption floor.

So another solution was found. A wonderful rescue that catered to special dogs like Logan agreed to take him. It was located about an hour away on a big farm with cows and horses, and it was quiet. Dogs were kept there until they were adopted.

I checked in from time to time by phone. I was afraid to go see Logan, because we had quite the connection, and I didn't want to confuse him. I already had my "three-pack" of doggies at home, or I would have taken him myself.

I was told Logan never showed any signs of aggression toward any dogs there. He made best friends with a cow during his stay, and eventually he found a loving home.

It was such a blessing to experience yet another happy ending that began with the love and brilliance of The World's Most Perfect Dog.

CHAPTER 25

MEANWHILE, BACK ON THE HOME FRONT

n mid-2013, around the time Logan was moved to his safe-haven rescue, Foxie began to show her age. She was fourteen years old. This little lady had been in my life for a long time, and we had gone through many chapters together.

She was always a bit timid, and she never really was the same after the death of her sister, Guera. But there was strength in her that kept her plugging along. Foxie adored Tampa, and she and Raja had gotten comfortable with each other over the years. They actually would snuggle together to nap sometimes. Raja respected her and pretty much let her be.

I had heard growlies between the girls over food and treats in the past. Tampa never got involved in that, but all three dogs were always separated at feeding time just as a precaution. In any household with more than one dog, that is generally just a good idea.

There was something else happening, though. Foxie's mind was going. I would see her circling in the kitchen sometimes as if she didn't know where she was. Then she would stop and stare at the wall, looking at nothing. Or perhaps she was looking to go "home," to be with Guera.

I would call to her, and she would tiptoe into the living room to say hello for just a minute, then go into the back room where her crate was and lie down.

So that's the way it was for a while. Foxie mostly just ate and hid in her back room. She loved the snow. When she watched it coming down as the season changed, I would let her go out and explore on her own. But her overall quality of life was fading. Tampa would go back and check in on her from time to time when she chose to go to her room. Then he would come to me and give me that look of his. In his ultimate wisdom, he was trying to tell me something.

"Mama, Foxie is getting tired."

His big, loving eyes were so warm. And his little doody lip was poking out. That is how he talked to me. Foxie wasn't suffering. I would not ever let that happen, but I knew decision time was coming. I soon found out I should have listened more closely to Tampa.

However, in all my life of owning dogs, I never had experienced the decision of whether or not to let them go. My first dog came to me when I was about three years old. I had a lifetime of dogs after that, but mostly they all just passed on their own very peacefully. That is, of course, with the exception of Guera. And her tragic death at such a young age probably left me hanging on to Foxie for too long.

By the spring of 2014, it was Foxie, God, or both that pushed me to that choice. This would be almost a year since I had begun to notice the changes in her. I had returned home one day after running a few errands. The routine stayed the same. Tampa and Raja went out first. Then my lil' old lady Foxie would go out on her own so she could have her privacy. That was the way she liked it.

Then it happened. All were back in the house, and I walked into the kitchen to unload the dishwasher. There was no food around—no rhyme or reason to what happened. Foxie just *launched* at Raja with no warning, and that was a horrifying thing to see. Raja did not want to fight. I pulled her away several times and she readily let go. Foxie just kept *charging*, even with me right there, and the dark look in her eyes was something I'd never seen in her before. She was also pooping and peeing all over herself as this continued to go on and on.

I was crying and becoming exhausted. I couldn't stop it. Raja was bigger and stronger, and she finally just had to defend herself. She managed to get a hold of Foxie's leg, and that is when it all stopped. Foxie gave up, and went to her room to lick her wound. It was a bad one.

I put Raja in the bathroom and quickly cleaned her up. She was very calm after such a violent episode, and amazingly came out of it with just some puncture wounds. Tampa gave me a very loving and knowing look, and I just asked him to watch over the house. He knew.

Then, with tears pouring down my cheeks, I bundled Foxie up in a towel to carry her to Dr. P's for the inevitable. I had called ahead sobbing, so they were expecting us.

I knew the answer, but I had to hear it from the vet team I trusted. It wasn't just the severe leg damage. What happened to Foxie mentally made everyone agree it was time. I won't lie. It doesn't help even when you do have that support. It is the most difficult thing to do in the world, but I had to set her free.

Foxie was the one who really had to tell me it was okay. They put a muzzle on her just as a precaution. She was not normally a kissy and overly affectionate dog. But as the vet team took care of their job, I held her little head and she managed to stick her tongue through the muzzle and lick my face.

"Thank you, Mama. I will see you again." She was peaceful. She knew where she was going. It was May 16, 2014 when she crossed over to Rainbow Bridge.

Many days of tears followed as I continued to beat myself up over this. I felt I should have seen it coming, but sometimes when a dog's mind goes, it snaps very quickly to aggression with no real warning. Some of you may have experienced it. The lesson is to not blame yourself. We do the very best we can by them when they are here, and we will make mistakes. I didn't want to let her go, so something else had to show me the way.

I think of Foxie now as she wanted to be. She is young again, and she is home with God and Guera, waiting to see all of us again someday.

CHAPTER 26

TAKING A
DIFFERENT PATH

*A*s Foxie's angel wings spread, yet another change was facing the family. The Humane League president, Joan, was retiring. I was so sad to see her go, because she was truly a delightful person who had the passion that was needed in her kind of job.

Things were also getting busier for me at the Q, which was good. However, it was starting to interfere with my availability to continue leading BARC. I still wanted to help the volunteers and the dogs, but my schedule was getting too jammed. So after a good bit of contemplation, I felt this was a cue for Tampa and me to start helping people and dogs from a different angle.

We tearfully said goodbye to our shelter friends in the summer of 2014. Of course, I kept in touch with a lot of the volunteers we had trained. They would touch base from time to time to ask questions about some dogs and to keep me up to date on how things were going. The dogs were in good hands. Several of the BARC "graduates" had become excellent handlers and dog walkers. So the program was still working through them.

Meanwhile, Tampa and I had decided to go into the business of private training. This way I could set my own schedule and work around my days at the Q.

"Hey, Tamp-Tamp. Let's go to work, just you and me, and help keep dogs from being dropped off at shelters in the first place! How does that sound?"

I got his smile and happy pant. He agreed. So off we went together, dropping off business cards everywhere I could think of. And, of course, Mr. Mayor was with me on every visit. The "master of first impressions" was my key to our new journey.

I had learned over the years that a lot of people tend to give up way too quickly on their dogs. Many of them did it tearfully when they surrendered a family member to a shelter. They had just run into a problem they could not fix by themselves and felt they had no other options. Tampa and I set out to change that.

Most of my client referrals came from Dr. P. He had known Tampa and me for years and had faith in the work we could do together. Now, I didn't always take my boy with me. Certain problems called for something I needed to do one-on-one with the family, but the visits with him were the most fun.

Mitzi "the bark fest dog" immediately comes to mind. She was a cute little Shih Tzu that belonged to an older couple who lived just around the corner from me. And boy, oh boy she was a barker! I determined pretty quickly that Mitzi wasn't aggressive. That was the good news. She was also not fearful. She was something in the middle, and I could certainly understand her parents being rattled by this, because she really did bark at *everything*!

I'm not talking about just people or cars. Mitzi barked at a shrub. She barked at mailboxes. She barked at bugs, garden hoses, garbage cans, the sun, the clouds, a mop, a plant, and a pillow that was propped up on the couch. I could go on forever with this. I will admit that it was rather amusing to me. It was just a little tiny bark. But I didn't have to live with her. So Tampa and I got our game faces on to help out.

We all went for a walk down the street together. It began very peacefully. And then came another moment that needed to be captured on video. In the middle of our walk, Mitzi just suddenly started barking at Tampa. The look on his face was priceless.

"Excuse me, young lady, are you in need of some assistance? If not, would you mind toning it down just a bit?"

Mitzi immediately stopped barking. I am not kidding. Now she tried it again several times, mind you, but Mr. Mayor corrected it with just a look. And after a good bit of repetition, it turned back into a peaceful walk. I think at that point Mitzi's parents wanted us to move in with them.

Seriously, I did determine that Mitzi was simply a nervous dog. Tampa had his quintessential, incredible calming effect on her, which he had on almost all dogs. But he couldn't be around all the time. I gave them some commands to use and suggestions on redirecting her—and they did talk with Dr. P about a mild sedative, which was also successful for them.

I giggled to myself as the thought came into my head:

"Wouldn't it be great if you could just bottle Tampa up, and prescribe him on a daily basis?!"

It was therapy that worked for Raja and me every day, that's for sure.

There are so many fun stories to tell, and wonderful dogs to talk about as Tampa and I continued to work together. We were, indeed, helping to keep dogs in their homes. He went with me on about half the visits, when dogs clearly needed help with socialization and a clear lesson in good manners. Mr. Mayor never disappointed. He was the teacher. Families from miles around appreciated him, and would never forget him. We would often get e-mails, cards, and doggie treats thanking us for our help. It was a very happy time.

CHAPTER 27

MR. JERRY

Of course, we couldn't let our friends at the nursing home down. The residents there counted on us. It made me sad that so many of them had to leave their own dogs with family or find other homes for them because they could no longer care for them.

Tampa was there to help fill that void. They rubbed his sweet face and talked about their furry babies from the past, and he always looked as if he was hanging on their every word. Some were more talkative than others. At times, they would just reach their fragile little hands out to touch his fur while they watched some television. It was his presence they wanted.

We had lots of regular friends, and there were always new residents coming in. One day, as I headed down our usual route, I came across a room with a name on the door I didn't recognize. The name was Jerry. I peeked my head in, because the door was open, and saw an elderly man who appeared to be sleeping. Three people were sitting with him who I assumed were family members, so I politely knocked.

"Good morning. Would Mr. Jerry like a visit from my dog?"

"Oh, yes! Please do come in. Jerry loves dogs."

Tampa and I eased into the room, and he immediately greeted the family members. They brightened up with the usual smiles and hugs at the sight of him. He accepted graciously, but I noted he had an intense interest in Mr. Jerry.

Now I may not have mentioned it before, but when you work in pet therapy, you do not ask about a resident's condition. If they offer it up, that is their choice. Otherwise, you are just there for a friendly visit. Mr. Jerry still seemed to be asleep, so I asked again.

"Are you sure Tampa can say hello to Mr. Jerry?"

"Oh yes. He isn't sleeping. He's just resting before lunch. Go ahead, please."

Since Mr. Jerry wasn't sitting upright, I had to ask if it was okay for Tampa to crawl up into the bed to get closer for some cuddle time. The family said that would be wonderful. I looked at Tampa.

"Up, up; easy now..."

He put his paws gently on the bed, and I lifted his back end up so he could lie close enough to Mr. Jerry to reach his face. He was a handsome elderly man with silver hair. He didn't seem to be in any pain or discomfort. His eyes were still closed, but he started to move a bit as he felt Tampa's presence.

Then, I could see the corners of Mr. Jerry's mouth turn up into a smile, and he reached his arms out to my boy. Tampa leaned in for a kiss, and then took his paws and lovingly wrapped them around Mr. Jerry's neck. They held each other. The elderly man's eyes fluttered a little, and he still had that smile on his face. Tampa held on gently. This was a moment. He had gotten up into beds before to give kisses and say hello, but I had never seen him do anything quite like this.

I saw and felt so much joy from Mr. Jerry as he quietly hugged my boy. It was beautiful. And then, something else happened. Tampa and I usually kept our visits with each resident to about ten minutes or so, then we would head on down the hallway to visit more friends. So I asked him to come with me.

"Time to go see more friends!"

Tampa didn't want to leave. He kept looking at me, and then at Mr. Jerry—his paws were still gently holding on. I let him stay a bit longer, but I eventually heard the attendants walking up and down the hallway letting everyone know it was almost time for lunch.

So my boy reluctantly had to let go. The family thanked us, and I told them we would be back very soon. Mr. Jerry never spoke a word. He didn't have to. And as we walked out of the room, Tampa kept looking back at him. It was rather odd to me, because he had never done that before either. I just guessed he had made a deep connection with this man, and I looked forward to our next visit.

As it turns out, the next day brought some extremely hot weather. I usually didn't visit back-to-back days, but Tampa and I were free, and I knew the residents wouldn't be able to go outside on the patio and enjoy the outdoors. It was just too hot for them. So we hopped in the car to go see our friends.

Miss Judith was one person we had visited often. She was the first door on the left in our hallway, so we stopped there immediately. She was a chatterbox and loved Mr. Mayor. As she scratched his ears and talked, she asked me a question.

"Did you two meet Jerry? The old gentleman just down the hall to the right?"

"Yes! We just met him yesterday. He and Tampa really connected. We're going to see him next."

Miss Judith sighed. "Christie, Jerry passed away unexpectedly last evening. He went very peacefully in his sleep."

I froze for just a moment. Then I gathered myself together, and told Miss Judith I was very sad to hear that. We talked a bit more and then said our usual goodbyes, because it was time to go visit some more friends.

"See you next week, Christie!" she said, sweetly waving and blowing us a kiss.

I slowly walked Tampa down the hallway. Then I sat in a chair with him beside me, just to take a minute to clear my head. I looked at him.

"You knew, didn't you? That's why you didn't want to leave Mr. Jerry. You knew."

He looked up at me with those warm, intelligent eyes, and nothing else needed to be said. I rubbed his soft ears as I thought about the time we had spent with Mr. Jerry. I should have been crying. Instead, I felt joy. During some of this sweet, elderly man's last hours on Earth, Tampa had given him something no one else could give him. I felt in my heart that Mr. Jerry had crossed over with a special, loving feeling that came from my once-in-a-lifetime dog.

CHAPTER 28

TIME TO SLOW IT DOWN

I saw it coming. We were sneaking toward the winter of 2015, and Tampa's age was starting to show. I knew when he was around three years old that he had slight signs of developing hip dysplasia. It was on his left side, and he would show a touch of an awkward gait on rare occasion. You had to look closely to even notice it. He also yelped one time when he landed wrong after jumping off the bed. My Florida vet X-rayed him at that time and told me not to worry. He said Tampa would very likely start to have problems with that only as he became much older.

I watched for it carefully all through his life's work. I kept his weight perfect. He showed me no pain or limping, so we barreled through SAR training, pet therapy, and training other dogs with no problems. I wouldn't let my boy hurt himself, and he was one that would let me know if something became too much for him.

Then one night, when he was almost fourteen years old, he let me know. Raja was already in bed with me. Tampa checked the perimeter of the house as usual, and then went to jump up on the bed to join us. He liked to sleep at the foot of the bed, facing the door so he could guard the family. So he jumped, and then I heard a "thunk," and a yelp.

I leapt out of bed and found him spread-eagled, all four legs going a different direction. His back end had given out on him, and the rest of him just kind of splatted on the hardwood floor. As usual, his loving eyes looked up at me.

"Can you help me, Mama?"

I gently lifted him up, and he walked on all fours with Raja and me out into the living room. I massaged his hips a bit, and that made him sleepy. I was trained in pet first aid, so I knew it wasn't an emergency. It was just a warning. I would need to make some changes around the house. For that night, I slept out on the couch so he wouldn't try to jump on my big bed again. Tampa had his dog bed, and Raja took the recliner.

At the time, I didn't realize that I would be a "couch crasher" for many months to come. I put some yoga mats and throw rugs all around the house so Tampa would have some traction, but he kept trying to jump on the bed at night before I got a chance to help him. Sometimes he made it—too many times, he didn't. So, it was back to the living room for all three of us.

Pain management came into play, of course. We tried several different meds, but Tampa was just not responding. They either didn't work, worked only temporarily, or made him sick. I needed to go a different route. He had good days and bad days, but I was on the hunt for something better.

Acupuncture! This never would have entered my mind if Dr. P had not suggested it. And to be honest, I wasn't sure if I really believed in it. But he referred me to an experienced person in this field of veterinary medicine, so I chose to give it a try. I wanted my boy comfortable.

Our first visit to Dr. Leslie was just a few days before Christmas in 2015. I liked her immediately, and of course, she fell in love with Mr. Mayor. He turned on the charm and kept the smile on his face as she placed the needles on different points all over his body.

"I have no idea what this is, Mama. It's weird. Am I doing okay?"

He reacted to some of the needles going in, but stayed pretty calm as Dr. Leslie and I talked and petted him. They stayed in for about twenty minutes. We expected him to lie down and begin to relax, because that is what most dogs do once this procedure starts to kick in.

Not Tampa! He followed Dr. Leslie all around her office, as if he was thanking her for trying to make him feel better. He was also on the hunt for a treat or two. He was no dummy. She petted him and gave him liver treats.

"He is a very special dog."

I can't tell you how many times I heard that during his lifetime, and I never got tired of it because it was true.

Now, once Dr. Leslie took the needles out and I put him in the car, he did crash. All the way home he slept. That was a good thing, and his movement was considerably better. He still had off and on days. Sometimes he would hop down the stairs to go out, others he would travel more carefully. But I was definitely seeing signs that he didn't have as much pain in his joints, so we continued our visits to Dr. Leslie about twice a month.

CHAPTER 29

HIS BUCKET LIST

$\mathcal{A}$s we turned the corner into 2016, Tampa and I faced some more challenges and changes. The floors at the nursing home were slippery for him in spots, and I didn't want him to try crawling up into beds to give hugs to residents because he could hurt himself. So I officially retired him from pet therapy and from training. It was sad for us, but it was the right thing to do. I continued to train dogs one-on-one to help people. It wasn't the same without him by my side, but I kept going.

Tampa was also showing some other signs of slowing down. His eyes had become somewhat cloudy, so I knew his vision was becoming impaired. I had to call to him more loudly to come back into the house because his hearing was going. And I just had this overall sense that we needed to collect as much quality time together as possible.

Who would have thought that a blizzard would be the first thing to check off on that bucket list? It was forecast to hit a day or so before I had to go on-air at QVC. And the way my job works, you must plan ahead. I had to be ready to go.

I set up a couple of overnight stays at a hotel near the Q. I would usually board both Raja and Tampa in such cases, but this time I wanted to take my boy with me. Raja was not exactly a "hotel type" dog. She would bark and go crazy when I had to go to work. I knew Tampa would just be himself.

This hotel would not normally accept dogs, but since Tampa was certified in SAR and pet therapy, they agreed. So I dropped Raja off with her friends and plenty of food at Dr. P's, and Tampa and I were off on our adventure together.

On January 22, 2016, we headed to the hotel. The storm was set to hit on the twenty-third—and boy, did it hit! The storm of storms! The snow was pouring down and blowing up from the ground all at the same time, swirling around like a white tornado. Tampa and I were tucked away in our room watching it together. I fed him his home-cooked meals that I had packed, and we managed to sleep safely and peacefully.

One of the best parts was that he did get to visit with people. That's what he loved. A team from the electric company was on standby in the lobby in case we lost power. They got to know my boy well, as I did have to take him out to go potty when necessary. Most of them were just sitting around kind of bored, so Mr. Mayor was happy to entertain them. They fed him little pieces of bacon and some egg from their breakfast plates. I usually didn't let that happen, but this was our special time together. I wanted him to enjoy it.

The other special part of this was Tampa's love for the snow. As things with the blizzard calmed down, I spent more time walking him around the hotel, embracing what was left behind. Well, my intent was to walk. The snow was up almost to my knees. It was up to Tampa's chest, but he was having a blast! He started leaping through it like a deer, bouncing almost as if he was on a trampoline. I worried about his hips, but he showed no pain. I believe that soft snow made him more buoyant, so the pressure was off his joints. He had so much fun, and I got so many Tampa smiles as he explored the beauty of it all. He looked like a puppy again.

When I did have to leave him for a longer period of time to go to work, I put QVC on the television in the hotel room.

"Watch Mama! You can watch Mama on TV!"

He was settled comfortably, and the parking lot had been cleared enough for me to get out very slowly. I made it to work, feeling secure that Tampa was peaceful in his hotel room. I was trying to focus on my job, but I was really just thinking about my boy.

And, apparently, he was thinking about me. Now, remember that his hearing was going—so when I came back into the hotel room after work, I did so quietly. He had actually managed to jump onto the bed and was watching QVC. He didn't initially hear me open the door. I took the moment in because it was so cute and just watched him staring at the TV. Then I called to him, and he hopped off the bed. He was having a good day, probably because the hotel room floor was all carpet and he could get some good softness and traction under his feet.

"Let's go play in the snow again, Mama!"

We went down, visited our friends in the lobby, then went out into the snow. It was still up to my knees in spots, and I did fall down a couple of times. When I did, Tampa came and poked his snow-covered nose in my face to make sure I was okay. We were laughing together.

Then it was dinnertime. We were both cold, tired, and hungry. I decided to do something special. There was an Outback Steakhouse next door that had reopened after the storm. I tucked him away in the room and walked over to get a doggie bag. One meal I ordered for myself, and then I politely asked if the chef could possibly make up something special for my boy. I home-cooked meals for all my dogs, so Tampa was accustomed to chicken, vegetables, sweet potato, etc. The chef was very kind, and did make Tampa's meal in a special skillet that hadn't been seasoned. I wanted to be sure his tummy didn't get upset.

"Room service!"

Oh, he could smell that perfectly cooked chicken and sweet potato as I came through the hotel room door. His eyes got big, and he was ready for his meal, specially prepared by a trained chef. I'm a good cook, but not as good as this. This was one more check off the bucket list.

We ate, and then we both crashed. It had been an adventure. He showed me so much life and love with meeting people and bouncing around in the snow. I truly wanted that feeling to last, but I knew there were many more challenges ahead.

CHAPTER 30

THE SUN BEGINS TO SET

*S*ometime during the late spring of 2016, I had moments when I was afraid to leave the house. I wasn't sure what I would find when I came home.

Tampa wasn't responding as well to the acupuncture. It helped some, but I could tell his back end was giving out on him. He was eating just fine. He would still slowly stroll around the yard, doing his job checking the perimeter. He could get up and down the few stairs to go in and out, but he just looked like he was getting tired.

There was also something else going on. The most brilliant dog I had ever known seemed to be losing part of his mind. Sometimes I would catch him staring at nothing, with a blank look on his face. Then I would whistle or clap my hands to kind of snap him out of it. He'd walk up to me and lean in for a scratch on the head and some kisses.

Now this was nothing like Foxie. I knew he was still connected enough to be that gentle, compassionate dog he always was. I wasn't worried that Tampa would suddenly turn aggressive by any means, but I didn't get as many of my Tampa smiles and happy pants. He would still let me help him up into the recliner so he could look out the picture window. That was his favorite view. I called it his "big boy" chair.

But I had to face the fact that my big boy was an old man now, and I could feel in my heart that I was eventually going to have to make a decision. I also knew, as always, that Tampa would let me know when. He did.

It hit him hard and fast, and it terrified me because I had no idea what I was looking at. One evening in early August, I was preparing dinner for him and Raja. I put her in her crate as usual, so she would leave his food alone. Then I put his bowl down and went to feed her.

When I walked back into the kitchen, he was lying down in front of his bowl. I had never seen him do that, but I thought maybe he was feeling a little weak and would be more comfortable eating that way. The problem was, he wouldn't eat. In the all the years I had this animal, I never once saw him turn down food. I sat on the floor and tried hand feeding, but he didn't respond. This was the beginning of something bad.

I got up for a minute and went into the bathroom to wash the tears off my face, and Tampa wanted to follow me as he always did, but his body wouldn't let him. My baby began thrashing all over the house as if he was having a seizure. He couldn't stand up but kept trying. His body was so out of control, slamming up against the walls, I thought he was going to break his neck.

I felt sick. I couldn't stop it. I had to do something. So I kept Raja tucked into her crate, and somehow managed to pick up this fifty-five-pound dog to carry him to the car. The animal emergency center with the best vets in the area was forty-five minutes away.

I put Tampa on the floor in front of the passenger seat so I could talk to him and try to calm him down, but he continued to thrash around trying to get up. The guilt just seeped through me, because I had to give him a strong command as I was driving to try to make him stop.

"Tampa, honey, *down*! Stay down for Mama, please!"

He had no idea what was going on. He would stop for a bit and then try again. His eyes darted back and forth, and he was obviously dizzy. I forced myself to breathe and hold back the tears, focusing on the road. We needed help fast.

CHAPTER 31

"IT'S CALLED VESTIBULAR DISEASE"

That is what the first vet said to me after she and her team examined Tampa. They, of course, sedated him so he would stop flailing around trying to stand up. She assured me he was resting at that point.

Up until that day I had no idea what vestibular disease was. For those who may not be familiar, it is a disorder that affects a dog's central nervous system. Actually, there are two strains: one is peripheral, the other is central.

Peripheral is related to an inner-ear problem. That is the most common form, and dogs usually recover in a matter of days with treatment. That was the good news.

The central is less common and much more serious. If that were to be his diagnosis, it would mean something was going on with his brain. That is not what you want to ever hear, especially with a dog that is almost fifteen years old.

The vet team began their plan. They explained that his eyes darting back and forth and the extreme dizziness should begin to subside after treatment with medication, if it was indeed peripheral. Of course, Tampa stayed sedated, and they had to give him fluids through an IV because he still wasn't eating or drinking water.

I peeked in on him when I left that night. He was lying down peacefully on a comfy bed. I didn't want to get too close, because I knew if he became aware of my presence he would start trying to get up again. They assured me their overnight staff would keep a close eye on him. This team would also draw blood and take X-rays of his internal organs to see if they could find anything else going on. I would get those results the next morning.

I was completely numb as I drove home. I had no idea how to feel. Raja came into play at that point. We needed each other. I had to get home to love on her because I knew she was already becoming confused. When I got home, I spent hours on the phone with a couple of very close friends. We talked until I was so exhausted I had to lie down on the couch. Raja was cuddled next to me. My throat was sore from talking and crying, so we rested.

The next morning, I drove in to see Tampa and talk to the vet team about his test results. The good news came first.

"His blood work is perfect, especially for an older dog. And we see nothing abnormal with his organs. You have taken great care of him."

I breathed a brief sigh of relief, but I could feel some tension and knew some more news was coming.

"Tampa is not responding to the meds we are giving him for his dizziness."

That meant he was still sedated. It also meant he was still on an IV drip because he refused to eat. They had even tried their own homemade chicken and rice. Nothing happened. He lifted his head to sniff at it, and then just laid back down.

Ultimately, over the next forty-eight hours, they determined that his vestibular disease was not an inner-ear problem. It was central vestibular disease. They suspected a lesion on the brain. Everything else had been ruled out. Tampa was fading away on me.

"We could run an MRI on him, but only if you want."

No. No way. I didn't think he would even survive that. They didn't recommend it. It was just their job to suggest that option.

"Can you give him another twenty-four hours, just to see if he starts to take a turn for the better?" I was on the phone from home at this moment.

"We will do everything we can to make him comfortable. But he is losing muscle mass very fast, and his organs will soon start to fail."

Then came the words I never wanted to hear. It was a horrifying nightmare that was coming true.

"Christie, if you want to be with him when he goes, you need to come back here now."

So, on August 6, 2016, I tucked Raja into her crate, and I got into my car. My mind was swirling with thoughts. I was going to fix this! The vets were wrong. I was going to see him and figure out exactly how to make him better. He was my child. He wasn't ready to leave his mama.

When I arrived at the hospital, the receptionist led me to a large, private room. There were couches, and pretty paintings on the wall. Some soft music was playing. I sat there and waited for them to bring Tampa to me.

Dr. Lisa was one of the four vets who had been attending to my boy. She rolled him into the room on a large bed. He was still sedated and gently strapped in so he couldn't move around too much.

"How is he?" I was crying and begging at this point. "Is there any chance that some other treatment will help him?"

"Christie, I've been doing this for twenty-five years. I promise you it is time for you to make this decision for your dog."

When Tampa heard our voices, he picked his head up. I'm sure he was aware I was there. I was also sure at that point that she was right. His eyes weren't just darting back and forth, they were also rotating around and around. His body looked tiny and frail to me. With my permission, she gave him another light dose of the sedative, and he put his head back down. It was time.

Dr. Lisa put her hand on my shoulder and handed me something.

"Here is a button to push when you are ready for me to come back in and take care of him. Take all the time you need, okay?"

I nodded. She left the room, and my tears were just pouring. I really did not want him to feel me crying. I wanted our last moments together to be about memories.

I put my face close to his and stroked his soft ears. He still smelled like fresh air and sunshine. I talked to him about our SAR days, and all the wonderful things he had done in his life. He was breathing quietly and his eyes were closed, but I knew he was listening. I promised him that Raja would take care of me and asked him not to worry. Then I wrapped my arms around him and pushed the button.

CHAPTER 32

THE PATH TO RAINBOW BRIDGE

"*E*very time I left, I was afraid it would be the last time I would ever see him."

Those words came from one of my best friends, Jake. He still lived in Sarasota, but would come up to Lancaster to visit the dogs and me from time to time. Jake is family to me. I've known him since 2004. And I will tell you this: we went through a lot of things together. There were plenty of emotional moments.

Throughout all those years, though, I never once heard or saw Jake cry. That is, until the day he found out Tampa was gone.

He called me that awful night and said he was sitting on the floor in his bathroom. It was such a full-blown cry that I couldn't even tell what he was saying, so we just cried together.

This was the most difficult journey I had ever faced in my life. I always believed our beloved pets crossed over and would be waiting for us at Rainbow Bridge—but the grief was taking over my faith. I was afraid. I didn't know how I was going to go on without Tampa.

Raja was very confused, but her strength kept her going. I felt like I was just running out of everything. I couldn't think. I was tired but couldn't sleep. What had I done to my baby? What did I do?

I pressed on with a lot of prayers, and my head began to clear somewhat when I realized the one thing I had asked of God.

"Please, let me be with Tampa when he goes. Don't let me come home and find that he left this world without me being there."

That prayer had been answered, and he was peaceful when he left. I did ask for him to be cremated so I could bring him home with me. The hospital also put together a lovely folding frame for me. One side had his paw print in it, the other told the story of Rainbow Bridge.

I slowly learned to breathe again, as I remembered how he made such a difference when he was here. My job at the Q offered a good distraction, although I was pretty much on auto-pilot when I was there. The friends I worked closely with knew what had happened to Tampa, and they helped me power through with a lot of hugs and comforting talks. I had to keep it together to go live on-air. Then I would break down when I was back home with Raja. That is the way it was for quite a while.

The grief hung on as I turned the corner into 2017. Raja had figured things out by then, and I really saw her grow up during that time. At ten years old, she was the kind of dog that still had plenty of puppy in her. But she had come to realize she needed to try to take care of Mama as Tampa had. She was calmer and very aware of my every move and emotion. She even moved to sleeping at the foot of the bed where Tampa used to sleep—facing the door to keep an eye on things.

I was still looking for something to pull me out of the pain. And one day, in early May of that year, I found it. It all began with a trip to Park